Things We Survive

—DARK SECRETS—

STEPHANIE J. CARR

© 2021 Stephanie Carr

All rights reserved.

No part of this publication in print or in electronic format may be reproduced, stored in a retrieval system, or transmitted in any form or by any means, electronic, mechanical, photocopying, recording, or otherwise without the prior written permission of the publisher.

The scanning, uploading, and distribution of this book without permission is a theft of the author's intellectual property. If you would like permission to use material from the book (other than for review purposes), please contact the publisher. Thank you for your support of the author's rights.

Distribution by Bublish, Inc.

eBook ISBN: 978-1-64704-360-5
Paperback ISBN: 978-1-64704-361-2
Hardcover ISBN: 978-1-64704-362-9

Cover design by 100Covers
Interior design by FormattedBooks

Dedications

I wish to dedicate this book to my loving family…to my amazing children—Savannah, my Jellybean; Buster; and Hannah—who show me strength every day. I wish I had your strength and courage. You all inspire me. To my precious grandbabies who give me so much joy and happiness and make life *fun*.

E.H.N.K.E.R.B.B. You all make life worth living. Nana Loves you all *forever*!

To my sisters and brothers, Piper, Dorothy, Jeffi, Lindsey, Justin, Jason, and Joseph, for all the laughs and love.

To my sister, Dorothy Carr, an amazing writer, editor, and marketing guru. Thank you for coaching me through this incredible journey.

To my friend, Rick Simon, for pushing me to become a writer and for his endless support and encouragement.

A special thank you to Sarah Williams of Mirror's Edge Photography for the Footprints cover photo.

To my sisters by choice, Peggy, Kathy, Kym, and Susan, for never letting me fall, even when I could not stand.

And to my dad, Joe Carr. Thanks for being the greatest example to me and my children, not only on how to be a parent, but how to be a person of forgiveness and love. You are truly my hero!

Till the next book…

Contents

Chapter 1	The Beginning—Life with Mother	1
Chapter 2	The Bathroom	5
Chapter 3	Richard	9
Chapter 4	My Dad	13
Chapter 5	Back to Hell	18
Chapter 6	Heartache	22
Chapter 7	Bye, Texas	24
Chapter 8	Hello, Cali	29
Chapter 9	Sharon	34
Chapter 10	I'm About to Die	40
Chapter 11	Harold	46
Chapter 12	Savannah	50
Chapter 13	Jellybean	57
Chapter 14	The Fall of Kenny	61
Chapter 15	Buster	65
Chapter 16	Abused Again	70
Chapter 17	Starting School	74
Chapter 18	Big Mistake	78
Chapter 19	Going Back to Cali	81
Chapter 20	Todd	85
Chapter 21	The Return	89
Chapter 22	Kallie and Peggy	92

Chapter 23	Independence Day	97
Chapter 24	Our New Life	99
Chapter 25	Enter #2	105
Chapter 26	Greatest Blessings	109
Chapter 27	Goodbye, Mother	113
Chapter 28	EJ and Hailey—OGs	118
Chapter 29	Justice, Finally—Kinda	120
Chapter 30	Kenny's Death	125
Chapter 31	Greatest Loss	128
Chapter 32	Baby Nahla	131
Chapter 33	Kylie	138
Chapter 34	Heart Attack	142
Chapter 35	Single	149
Chapter 36	Hannah	151
Chapter 37	Grace, Riley, and Button	154
Chapter 38	When Will I Ever Learn?	161
Chapter 39	Mark	167
Chapter 40	Crushing Revelations	170
Chapter 41	Birdie Belle	177
Chapter 42	Brain Surgery	180
Chapter 43	Aftermath and Arraignment	190
Chapter 44	Siblings	193
Chapter 45	Losing Joan	200
Chapter 46	Family First	207
Chapter 47	Lessons Learned	210

1

The Beginning—
Life with Mother

The weather is perfect as I sit on my beach looking out at the beautiful Pacific Ocean, which is one of my favorite places. The sun is warm, but not hot; it's seldom hot in Shell Beach. It can be cold and overcast, especially in the summer. But today is delightful.

It has become a day of reflection as I watch my youngest granddaughters blissfully play in the waves. I feel so blessed that they have never endured real pain. Sure, they have felt pains from cuts and falls, the regular childhood stuff, but not the pain of abuse, fear, regret, and genuine sadness. Thank you, Heavenly Father, for keeping them safe from the evil of this world. My son and daughter-in-law have done an amazing job as parents. It makes me proud of my son and his choice of wife, Hannah, who has become not only my daughter but one of my best friends.

My youngest granddaughter, one year old Birdie, squeals from the thrill of outrunning a wave, one that in her mind, would surely sweep her out to sea, never to be seen again. As she trips while outrunning the killer wave, scraping her knee, she looks up and sees me, her Nana. The moment our eyes meet, she begins to cry, knowing I will come and scoop her up, rescuing her from the killer wave and from surely bleeding to death from the miniscule scrape on her knee. So I go to my sweet angel, pick her up, hug her, and give her the cuddles needed to reassure her that everything is going to be fine. I dust the sand off her knee, kissing it and her, and then come the tickles, which are sure to make her laugh. Birdie is all healed with a simple kiss, cuddle, and tickle. A few giggles later, she is off and running again, rejoining her big sister Button in the daredevil act of outrunning the killer waves. Wanting to keep up with her sister, even though the waves terrify her, she knows that she is safe, as Mom and Nana are watching.

Sitting myself down, I realized I did not recall having that feeling, that sense of security, with my own mother. I do not ever remember having fun days like this with my family, never mind a healing kiss or snuggle from my mother. She was not the affectionate type nor one to take us kids on an adventure just for fun. She had undiagnosed and untreated bipolar disorder and, back in the seventies, people did not discuss it, but rather chose to ignore it. If you had a family member that was "off," people just felt bad for you but never wanted to help or get involved with that kind of illness.

I used to fear the sound of my mother's voice because it usually meant I was about to "get it!" As a child, I never could understand her nor why she did the things she did. They did not make sense to me and I did not know if it was me or her that was "off." I kinda knew she was the one that was off because my friends' moms were not crazy like mine. I would watch the other moms show their kids love and affection. I must have seemed like a sad little girl to the other moms, as I would stare at their interactions, especially the hugs, the physical touch between my friends and their moms. My best friend Dorothy's mom even hugged me when she would see me. It felt warm and comforting; it was something that I craved even though it was unfamiliar.

Dorothy's family was the family I wanted. They seemed like a dream to me. Mom and dad, little brother Joseph, and a dog, a pure white German Shepherd named Snowflake. I remember feeling that if I wished hard enough, maybe God would make me part of their family. Her dad, Joe, was kind and always laughed and made me laugh. I would watch him hug his children and longed for that kind of love and affection. The pesky little brother was even sweet. My little brother was just a baby, but I wanted to take him and my little sister and be part of this family where there was love and comfort, unlike my mother and my father who obviously did not love me.

Dorothy and her family ended up moving to California, and I was devastated. In my short life, it was one of the greatest feelings of loss I'd yet to endure. I sobbed when I heard the news and wished I could hide in their car and go with them. *If I could just find my way to their house. Why had I not watched closer how to get there?* They left and I cried and cried. Back then, once someone was gone, they were truly gone. We did not have cell phones or social media. I felt lost.

Because my mother's crazy would change daily, it was difficult to predict what would set her off. I was convinced she despised me and everything about me, which was confirmed on the days she would rant that she "wished I'd never been born." Those days would sometimes be followed by days of exuberance, sheer joy. Like making ice cream sundaes and squirting loads of whipped cream on top and laughing. Then, some days she would be so sad, she could not get out of bed or even make eye contact with anyone. Then there were her evil days. For me, these were her worst days, almost like she was an alien impersonating a human. Her eyes even looked different on these days. There was no pattern, no trigger, just constant change and inconsistency. So, as a first grader, I was confused and sad a lot. I knew what the normal moms were like and I wanted a normal mom. I wanted a *normal* life!

Baby Stephanie

2
The Bathroom

I'm not sure how old I was exactly—I think maybe six or seven—but I remember we were spending the night with our grandparents. During the night, I was woken up by my grandpa, who took me and my little sister into the bathroom. He held his index finger to his lips as if to shush us, like we were about to get a treat, one that the boys were not getting, and that excited me. It was early in the morning, and still dark out so I was struggling to keep both eyes open. Grandpa whispered that we were going to try something and if we did not like it, we could spit it out. I could not imagine what sort of treat we were going to get in the bathroom so early in the morning, when everyone was asleep.

I was so young and could not understand why he started reaching into his pajama pants. He was sitting at the edge of the tub; my sister and I were on our knees on the floor. And then he pulled his penis out. I was in shock, embarrassed, and tried to look away, but he grabbed my face and turned it back to where it was directly in front of him. I had never seen a penis and had no idea what sort of evil I was about to experience.

My grandpa then put his penis on my mouth and I was terrified. I sat there, scared and tight-lipped, and he whispered, "open your mouth, lick your lips." My heart hurt like someone was squeezing it from inside. The floor was cold and I could smell the water from the drain of the tub and it smelled like moss. His penis smelled awful, like dirty sweat and urine. I could feel my sister trembling, like she was cold. I'm pretty sure she was crying, but I could not hear her. All I could hear was the pounding of my heart and I was convinced that it might just burst or stop, and I was ok with that, except for thinking that if I died, my sister would be all alone. Somehow, I had to protect my baby sister.

I knew this was wrong, not because I was ever taken aside and told that grown men did not do this to little girls, but I knew in my young heart it was wrong…the heart that was about to burst. I wanted to throw up, to scream. I could not do anything but let him do what he was doing. I was paralyzed with fear. I did as I was told till he was done. When he started ejaculating in my mouth, it startled me, and I pulled away, choking. He was so angry that he grabbed my sister and finished in my sister's mouth.

He asked, "don't you like it?" I shook my head no, and he was pissed at me and said to spit it out but that I would learn to love it. What would make that evil man ask a child if she liked it? He then told us to never speak about it again or we would be in so much trouble. We were led back to bed and I pulled my sister close and she was silent and still. Trying to now keep my sister safe, I put her on the side closest to the wall.

I asked God to protect my sister and never let that happen again. I prayed for God to make me braver so I could protect her.

I prayed that she and God would forgive me for not protecting her. I felt shame, I felt disgusted with myself, like I was a bad girl, a dirty girl. I truly was that unloved child I had always believed myself to be.

As I laid there terrified, I heard his words over and over, "open your mouth, lick your lips"…"you will learn to love it." I started to cry because that must mean he was going to do it again. I knew I never wanted to go there again but I did not ever get a say or opinion.

The second time it happened, I told grandpa that my sister could not do it because her mouth was too little and she got so sick last time. So he left her alone. She laid on the floor with her head in my lap as I covered her eyes with my hand. I could feel her shaking and smell the moss smell of the tub again, and him, the smell of dirty sweat and urine. I could still only hear my heart pounding but I could feel my sister's tears on my legs, which were soaking through my pajamas. This was something else people just did not talk about back then, molestation. I never spoke about it when it happened but felt that I had learned how to protect my little sister from it and he seemed satisfied to just abuse me from that point forward.

The helplessness and disgust I felt was overwhelming. I felt shame and sadness. Why was I ashamed? I was a baby and that grown man was the one that should feel the shame, but he liked it, and he knew he could intimidate me into silence. And silence is what he got. I never spoke about it. I never told anyone and I was hoping my baby sister would forget about it. She was so little. He would act like nothing ever happened. I could not make eye contact with him. It made me feel guilty. Not sure why I felt guilt. I was a baby and I had no choice in the abuse. If I had a choice in the matter, I would never go to their house again. If I really had my choice, I would make him go to jail forever, or die.

As a child, I'd had my innocence ripped away from me and replaced with fear. I knew that it was wrong, I was six or seven and I knew things most six or seven-year-old little girls should not know. I knew what a penis looked like and what it did and what it smelled and tasted like. Well, I knew what his smelled like and it disgusted me. As an adult, it infuriates me that that man did that to me and my sister. He robbed us of an innocent childhood. What he did to us has left us with emotional scars that will follow us our entire lives.

3

Richard

When I was born, I was given my mother's husband's last name and was told he was my father. He was not, but I did not know that. Mother's husband Bob was not a loving, affectionate man. I don't remember even getting a hug from him, a comforting moment, or an *I love you*. I honestly don't know if he ever even spoke to me. Maybe he did know I was not his child.

Looking back now, I'm sure it was obvious to outsiders from the beginning. My older brother, Samuel, and younger sister, Jeffi, were brunettes with brown eyes, olive complexions, and heavy physiques. Yet, here I was with blonde hair and blue eyes and stick-thin, a feature I obviously outgrew. I did not blend in back then but never questioned otherwise. My older brother used to tell me that they found me out by the mailbox as I got older. It almost seemed possible, as I never felt like part of the family.

Mother and Bob divorced and my mom married a wonderful man, Richard. Richard and mother had another brother for me, Jason, and I adored him. I promised to always take care of him and show him love, even if our mother did not. My baby brother Jason was a bright light in my life and he loved me and I knew he loved me. Richard was strict but kind and he showed me love. He would put me in his lap and hug me and say, "I love you." I soaked it up. I even called him Dad.

Mother was still "off," but it helped having dad around to protect me. But I still had to endure Mother and her "crazy," especially when dad was not home. My older brother picked up on mother's meanness and began picking on me, too. He would tell mother things to get me in trouble. He learned fast that he could blame everything on me, even when I saw him do certain things, and mother would totally take his word for it and I would get beat.

He had the same evil eye Mother would get and he would watch and smile when I was being punished. And by punished, I mean *beat*, I was never spanked; I was beat.

I vividly remember in fourth grade, we were sitting at a table and I could tell when Mother sat down that she was in an evil mood. It was hard to miss because her eyes changed and she would speak through clenched teeth, enunciating every word like there was a pause between each word. So at the dinner table, Mother asked, "whose turn is it to do the dishes?" My older brother, for reasons only known to him, said, "it's Steph's turn, she made me take her turn yesterday, and she said it was stupid that you make us take turns and that you're too lazy to do it yourself."

Wait, *what*? First off, he was two years older than me and outweighed me by a hundred pounds. I'd never been able to nor ever thought to try to *make* him do anything. Second, I never said that. But, needless to say, my mother did not take that well and she backhanded me so hard, my chair flipped backwards and I hit the wall with the back of my head. As I was lying there on the floor, seeing stars, mouth full of blood, my mother was screaming, "how dare you say I was stupid; she was educated and I was the stupid one," and then said her favorite line, "I wish you were never born." All I could think was, "me, too, mother, me, too, I wish I was never born." Had I ever said what was going through my brain, I would have been beat to death. So, I just kept it all locked up in my head and I refused to shed any tears; I'd never give her the satisfaction of seeing me cry.

Meanwhile, my older brother was still sitting at his place at the table eating and grinning as if he enjoyed watching me get beaten. I tried to defend myself by saying that "I did not say any of that," but it got me another punch to the face, lip split open, more blood in my mouth. So, when I was told to get up and Mother asked, "what did I have to say for myself," I just said I was sorry. There was no use trying to defend myself against the mother that did not love me and the brother that hated me.

As usual, I cleaned myself up and was sent to my room so I could "think about it," think about what being a liar gets me. I spent a lot of time in my room, *"thinking about it!"* I remember my dad Richard coming home a lot of times and asking, "what did you do?" I wanted to shout "*nothing*, your crazy wife beat the crap out of me for nothing." But I was too terrified of what mother would do to me when he wasn't there or if my older brother would hear me by eavesdropping. I already got beat for things he made up. I could not imagine what awaited me if I actually did or said something against my mother. Truly I felt that she would one day go too far and kill me. I just hoped it would not be in front of my little brother or sister.

I would willingly take the blame for anything that might get them disciplined. mother was not as hard on them but they saw the things she did to me, so there was fear in them. Our older brother was very manipulative and could turn anything against us, making himself out to be innocent. He wasn't. In turn, I felt it was my job to protect them.

Having failed my sister years earlier when we lived near Grandpa, I did not want to fail my little brother or sister again.

Our family felt like two families forced together. Mother and my older brother Sam, and me and my little brother Jason, and little sister Jeffi. Although it was apparent that mom loved my little brother and sister, they could still be under attack if my older brother decided he wanted them punished. Luckily for them, I was the focus of his and mother's hatred.

4

My Dad

When I was ten, my mother sat me down at the kitchen table and told me some shocking news, way too complex for a ten-year-old's brain to process. She said that my dad was not my real dad, that my real dad was Joe. Wait, what? Joe? My best friend from first grade, Dorothy's dad, that Joe? The man I wished was my dad? He was really my real dad?

How was that possible? I remember being confused but thrilled. It's a lot for a ten-year-old to absorb. My mother said I was going to fly to California to see him for a week. I began to pray, "Please God, let them want to keep me." If I never have to see my mother and older brother again, I would be ok with that.

As an adult all these years later, as I type that, I know it seems cold. But I had never felt love from my mother or brother. I felt like the unwanted, broken child-turned-slave. I had been abused by my mother all my life and really would not miss her or my brother at all. I would miss my little brother and little sister but maybe I could be brave and tell *my* dad about what mother had been doing to me and he would help me rescue them. The space between Texas and California seemed like a safe distance, safe enough to share the secrets I kept.

In the week between finding out about my *real* dad and getting on the plane, my mother was nice to me. It was weird and even more confusing than my young brain could process. Why was she being kind? Why was she not smacking the shit out of me when my older brother would blame me for something he did? I understand it now, because she did not want me to go to California bruised or with a split lip. I think she wanted me to *think* she loved me and she wanted to keep me from saying anything negative to *my* dad.

My dad. . . how was this happening? I had prayed for this and wished for it since I was in first grade and Dorothy was in kindergarten and we were best friends from the moment we met at Amherst Street School. I thought maybe I had prayed and wished hard enough that I was being blessed with an amazing family that would love me. I could not wait to get to California.

My time in California with my dad and best friend-turned-sister, brother Joseph, and stepmom was amazing. I felt like I had died and gone to heaven. I felt like a part of a family; I felt loved and wanted for the first time in my life. While there, I was never beaten, never yelled at, never made to feel less than an unwanted stray dog. I was *loved*, I was wanted, I was a good girl and no one knew the dirty details of my past. All the terrible memories were there, but they were not my reality in California.

We swam and played every day, all day. We did not have to do chores. I took about a hundred pictures of palm trees. I was even asked what I wanted on my sandwich at lunch, which may seem weird to some but I had never been given an option before. My stepmom Jan was a sweet, wonderful woman who showed me more of a mother's love than I had ever felt before. She and my dad tucked me and my sister in at night and said I love you every day. And the hugs, I knew I would never in my whole life be hugged as much as I was that week in California. And it felt wonderful. To this day, I am a hugger.

I remember my last night in California; I did not want to leave the next day. I wanted to beg them to let me stay. They kept talking about my "next visit" but I did not want to visit; I wanted to stay permanently. I almost started to cry and tell my dad what my mother was doing to me. He had no clue what I was holding back. He must have just thought I was sad to leave or a weird emotional kid. He hugged me and told me that the next visit would have to be longer. I remember asking him through tears, "really?" and he said, "of course, that he would talk to my mom about getting another visit in before the end of summer." I believed that he truly wanted me to come back soon.

In the editing of this manuscript, Dorothy wrote:
Not that I'm a counselor but do you realize this is the first time thus far you used the word believe - after reading this so many times, as a child you did not have a reason to believe in anything until you found your real family - through them you began to believe - you began to have faith, to trust that your life was precious that you were meant to be loved and that you were good. That you were wanted.
I had to add her thoughts as I had not realized it till then but this is exactly how it felt. My family loved me

and I believed in a family's love now, since discovering they were mine. My dad, my sister, my brother, my stepmom. How blessed I felt for the first time in my life.

As I was flying back to the reality of my life in Texas, I began to feel that unwanted child once again take hold and I cried and prayed for God to not send me back. I felt like a scared little girl that could not stand up to her mother or tell my dad what was happening. Why could I not be brave? I prayed for God to make me brave. I begged for forgiveness for not protecting my sister back in that bathroom, I prayed for forgiveness for what happened in there. When I was little, I still felt like it was my fault and I felt like I had done something wrong.

I wish I could go back and talk to that scared broken abused little girl and tell her that it was not her fault and that God would never stop loving her because of what bad people did to her. I would tell her that she was brave and strong and to never give up!

I remember wondering why my mother would allow me to go on such a wonderful trip. Maybe she did love me in some weird way. Then, when I got back to Texas, there were no hugs, no *I'm so happy to see you* from my mother or older brother. Mother picked me up and yelled at me before we even got in the car as I wasn't walking fast enough for her liking. Once home, my little sister and brother hugged me and wanted to hear about California. Convinced, like I was, that there were movie stars next door to everyone in California, their questions spilled out. But that was immediately squashed when Mother told me to wash the dishes before I unpacked my bag. And to hurry because it was almost bedtime. My reality had once again returned.

———————— THINGS WE SURVIVE ————————

5

Back to Hell

I fell back in line, doing as I was told without question. My older brother picked up where he left off, blaming me for anything and everything, setting me up to have my ass kicked at least once a week. It was easier for me to keep my mouth shut and never speak unless I was apologizing for something I did not do or say. I could never say what my mother wanted me to say. So, I would only speak when I was asked a question and still found myself in trouble a lot, with her backhand across my face.

Mothers newest form of torture was to put me "up against the wall." I used to dread hearing that, "up against the wall." She would make me stand facing the wall, about twelve inches from it, while standing on my tippy toes with my feet spread apart and my hands against the wall, supported only by my fingertips. If I rested my fingers by having my whole palms on the wall or if I rested on my whole foot instead of on the tip of my toes, I would get the belt across my backside somewhere. She was a bad aim because she would hit me with that belt anywhere from the back of my legs up to my neck. I would have to stand there for hours sometimes. It may not sound hard, but try it and imagine standing there for hours.

I never did get to go back to California that summer and feared that I would never be allowed to again. I often dreamed about the time I had in California with the family that loved me.

School was about to start and we went to the doctor for check-ups. I was apparently found to be anemic, which meant mother was pissed at me. "Why could I not be perfect, why did I make her life so miserable," she asked. She decided that since I was anemic, I needed to eat only liver or fish. I did not like either, but every day I was given liver or fish to eat. If I did not finish my dinner, it would then become my breakfast. I grew to *hate* liver and fish.

One time, I was gagging so bad I threw up on my plate and my mother told me, "I had to eat it or I would be on the wall until I ate it *all*." I thought I would die if I was forced to eat this vomit on my plate; I tried my best but kept gagging. I was trying to let it slide down my arm, safely hidden in my sleeve. I don't know how I managed to eat enough of my own puke to satisfy my tormentor. But she finally said, disgusted, like I had *failed* her, to "clean up the rest and go to bed." I cleaned it up, retching, but determined to not throw up anymore. I made sure to get rid of it all so I wouldn't be forced to eat it for breakfast. Eating fish for breakfast was bad enough but if I had to eat fish throw-up again, I would surely die.

I went to the bathroom and threw up as quietly as I could. I washed my face and brushed my teeth. I will never forget the taste in my mouth and the evil in her eyes as I was forced to do something so disgusting. Who does that to her own child? I felt like I just wanted to die. I promised that if I ever had kids, I would *never* make them eat liver, fish, or anything they did not like, and *never ever* make them eat their own vomit.

My stomach was empty and aching but I knew that there would be nothing to eat until breakfast and I was praying it was not liver or fish. As I laid there quietly, waiting for my little sister to come in for bed and at least have someone to talk to, I cried and prayed and daydreamed about being in California with my dad. I wasn't sure what being anemic meant but maybe my dad would hear about it and come save me, or, maybe I could die and go to heaven.

My little sister came in and snuck a piece of bread with peanut butter on it. She handed it to me and said to eat it quickly before mother came in. I inhaled it and rolled on my side when she came in as I was afraid she would smell the peanut butter and beat me for sneaking food, Or worse, beat my sister for helping me, so I held my breath. I was so upset at my mother, I told myself that if she would have started beating my sister I was determined to jump up and hit her back and take my sister and run away. I laid as still as possible and she never even acknowledged me. When she left the room, turning off the light, my sister climbed up to the top bunk and climbed under the covers with me and draped her arm over me and said, "I love you, Teff." I told her that I loved her too and quietly began to cry because I did not want my little sister to hear me and also cry. She would cry when she saw me cry and I did not want to make her cry ever again.

I quickly learned to eat what mother gave me and go throw up quietly in the bathroom if I could not keep it down. My little sister would sneak me in food if I got sick and was hungry or if they had dessert I wasn't allowed to have. I feel like my little sister probably saved my life during that time.

I went to bed hungry a lot, but totally appreciated the food my sister snuck in for me. I knew that when I grew up and had kids, I would *never* make them eat anything they did not like. That they would never go to bed hungry or without knowing they were loved. As an adult, I always cook too much food and always have plenty of leftovers. My kids ate what they liked and were never forced to eat anything they did not like. I was always obsessed with making sure we had plenty of food in the house. I can admit that I'm kind of a food hoarder and overbuy groceries. I'm certain it came from the memories of this time in my life.

6

Heartache

Safely back on my beach with my family, having a beautiful beach day, I reached into the ice chest for a cold drink as my granddaughters came running up to our blankets and beach chairs, asking for snacks. I opened the bag of treats and the ice chest, asking what they would like. Their choice. My daughter-in-law and I had delicious sandwiches, chips, snacks, and fruit. I feel blessed that she is such a wonderful mom and loves her babies. She treats them like a loving mother should and allows me so much time with them. I am so happy that they have never had to feel the kind of pain I endured at the hands of my own mother.

One day, I remember my mother saying that my older brother was going away for a few weeks. I remember being so happy, I felt like I would get into less trouble with him gone. Maybe I would even get lucky and he would never come back. I was quietly celebrating and I'm sure I was smiling, something I rarely did. Then the bomb was dropped. He was going to California. Wait, what? Not only was he going to California, but he was going to *my dad's* house. Why *my* dad?

God, please don't let it be true. Why was he going to *my* dad's house and why for a few weeks, he is *my* dad? Oh, God, please don't let him be my dad's child, too. How on earth could there be this many secrets in one family? Luckily, I learned that he was *not* my dad's son, but I was still devastated, that was *my dad*, and my dad did not like mean boys that lied. Why not send me? Why send him? I know now how irrational it was to be so panicked, but I was afraid that my brother would turn my dad against me. Jealousy engulfed me like a wildfire burning my whole body that could not be extinguished.

I cried a lot at night knowing my brother was with *my* dad and probably doing his best to turn him against me, telling lies and making dad believe that he was perfect, and I was bad. But there was nothing I could do. I felt helpless and sad. Why was he there for so long? As the days turned to weeks and weeks turned into months, I was convinced that my brother had won my dad over and he had decided to keep my brother. I was so sad that he had not made that decision with me. Maybe my dad felt the same way about me now that my mother did, that he wished I was never born. Maybe I was just bad and no one wanted me. I felt such heartache, I just wanted to die so I wouldn't feel that pain in my heart anymore.

Now, as an adult, I know that was the farthest thing from the truth but as a child my heart was crushed, and I felt such a great loss and overwhelming sadness.

7

Bye, Texas

After a few months of my brother being in California with *my* dad, my world was about to change again. One day, I got up and started getting ready for school. I was in the fourth grade and not a terribly good student, but I preferred to be at school where I could eat normal food and not be punished for a wrong look. I just enjoyed being away from my mom. I was in the bathroom brushing my teeth and mother came in and put her hand on my forehead, something she never did, so I flinched. She said I felt feverish. I felt fine but did not speak to say I was fine; I knew better. But I was upset because I knew it meant I was going to be home with her all day. I was pissed because I was going to miss out on pizza day at school and chocolate milk.

God knows what she was planning. She led me to the living room and lovingly helped me to lay down on the couch and put a pillow under my head and covered me with a blanket. I was confused but laid there quietly.

She put the TV on and went into the kitchen and told my dad that I was sick. He was grabbing his lunch and on his way out the door when he bent over and kissed my forehead and said, "feel better pumpkin, I love you." And he left for work.

Mother watched as he drove away and *instantly*, as soon as his vehicle disappeared around the corner, life changed. Mother started barking orders. I was to pack a trash bag with as many of my brother's and sisters' clothes as I could, then I was to put the bags in my room and shut the door. Once finished, I was to lay back on the couch and not say anything, especially if dad came home.

Fear, confusion, and sadness. What the hell was going on? I did as I was told. I went to the kitchen and got the trash bags. I went to my brother's room first and put all his clothes in the bag and snuck in a few of his favorite toys, wrapping them up in each of his shirts. I know I was probably going to be punished for it but I wasn't sure where my baby brother was going and I wanted him to at least have a few of his favorite things. Dragging the full bag into my room, I heard a noise coming from the front of the house, so I ran to the living room, jumped on the couch, and covered up. I was not afraid of my stepdad but I was afraid I was going to have to lie to him and I was not sure I could without crying. So I pretended to be asleep for several minutes.

As I lay there, I realized that my bedroom door was not closed and the bag could easily be seen. My heart pounded from running around but I realized that my stepdad was not there—it was the neighbors leaving for work. I went back to my room and started packing a bag for my sister the same way I did for my brother, hiding toys she liked rolled in her clothes. I started wondering where they were going? Why had mom not said to pack a bag of my clothes? Was she taking my little brother and sister away forever, was she leaving me here with my stepdad? That would be OK with me, except I would miss my baby brother and sister. I started questioning if mom had said to pack a bag for me as well, but no, she had not, I was sure of it, almost.

I had learned to do *exactly* as she told me to, nothing more because that would be assuming I was smarter than her and she made it a point to point out that she was smart and I was stupid every day of my life. But what if she had told me to pack my own bag and I was not listening close enough? So I grabbed another bag and put several of my clothes in it and put it in my closet just in case she hadn't told me to pack a bag for myself. Then, if I started to get in trouble for not doing it, I would produce the bag and avoid a beating. I only had a few outfits in the bag and mother scared the crap out of me when she came bursting through the front door, yelling at me to grab the bags. I dragged the bags out to the front door and, as I emerged from the house, I saw a tiny U-Haul attached to her car.

My brother and sister were in the back seat of her car looking as confused as I was. We were apparently going somewhere but no one knew where. Amidst a flurry of yelling, she opened the garage and pointed to several boxes covered with a tarp in the corner. We started loading them into the U-Haul, along with some boxes from her room. She tried to put the kitchen table in but it wouldn't fit, so she left it in the front yard. I ran into the house, grabbed my bag of clothes, a pillow for my brother, sister, and myself. I stuffed my brother's stuffed bunny from his bed into his pillow. I grabbed a blanket for each of us and took them out to the car.

Mother continued to yell like it was a race of some sort. She had all those boxes packed and ready? Why? Why was it such a race? Was dad going to be home in time to go or was he meeting us wherever we were going? Should I have packed dad a bag? I kept loading the mysterious boxes into the U-Haul till they were all in and we were off. But to where? I did not know and I was scared to ask.

My baby brother finally asked, "where are we going, mom?" Finally!!! I was dying to know what the hell was happening. Mother said, "California." California? Closer to my dad? I was thrilled. Maybe I could see my dad. I would have to pay attention to how to get to his house so I could run away there some day when I got the nerve. Now I began to pray that my brother had not turned my dad against me. I prayed he still loved me.

After several miles of elation over the road trip we were embarking on, my baby brother asked another question that I will hear in my memory forever. "Mom, is daddy coming to California, too?" Mother then told her five-year-old child, "no, we are going to California to be safe from your dad!" Safe *from* dad? The only one we need protection from is you, lady.

My baby brother started to cry, saying he wanted his daddy. My heart was breaking for my brother and for this wonderful man that had shown me love since the day I met him. I cried silently thinking about him coming home to the kitchen table overturned in the front yard and no family. I had loved this sweet, wonderful man for five years; I called him Dad. I felt the love of a parent from him, always. I wanted to jump out of the car and stay there with him. At least I could be safe from my mom's abuse and dad wouldn't be alone. But I was scared, like I always was. I could just hope to see my real dad and hope to be able to somehow end up with him.

Mother yelled at my baby brother to be quiet and stop crying. She was screaming at him, "your daddy is mean and abused us all and we are running away to be safe." He quieted a bit but continued to sob. I reached in the pillow I had grabbed for him and pulled out the stuffed bunny he loved. I gave it to him so he could snuggle it and not be so sad. I pulled him close and whispered in his ear that daddy loves you and he would see his dad again. Putting his pillow on my lap and then his tiny head, he cried himself to sleep as I scratched his back.

We got as far as El Paso and mother stopped at an airport. We were all exhausted and still unsure what was happening. We all got out of the car and as we were walking into the airport, Mother said we were picking up my dad so he could help us drive to California. Wait, what? *My* dad?

I was excited to see my dad, but I was fearful that my brother had turned him against me. What lies could he have told in his time in California with *my* family? I was silently praying that he still loved me. I was so quiet while we waited. I fell asleep and dreamed that mother was hitting me and my dad stood in between us and stopped her and took me into his arms and said that she would never beat me again.

I woke up to see my dad walking towards me. I was asleep on the floor in an airport terminal and as soon as I saw him, I sat up, rubbed my eyes and knew, as soon as I saw his face and he saw mine, that he still loved me. His face lit up with the biggest smile. I jumped up and ran to him, crying. I was so thankful that, no matter how bad I was or how unlovable, according to my mother, *my* dad still loved me. Thank you, God!

Off we went to California.

8

Hello, Cali

I had learned to always be quiet and not ask questions. I barely made eye contact with people, but with my dad, I was able to speak and laugh and smile. It was weird when we first got to California. My dad and stepmom had gotten a divorce and that made me very sad, but I was still able to see Jan from time to time, thank God, because I loved her and wished she was my mom. As the days passed, I learned what a master manipulator my mother was. She had the exit from Texas all planned for months. When she sent my brother to California, she had told my dad that my stepdad was beating my brother, so my dad offered to take him in. While still in Texas, my mother told my stepdad that my older brother was troubled and increasingly violent towards us kids, so she was sending him to stay with my dad to protect us.

She told my dad that my stepdad was beating her and us kids and she was in fear for our lives, so he told her to come to California. The only beating that was going on was by her to me. If my stepdad ever saw her get violent, he would step in and protect me.

Mother struggled with allowing me the freedom to be a kid, to laugh and smile and climb up in my dad's lap and get hugs and snuggles. She could not beat me in front of my dad and I knew it. I could see her seething with anger sometimes because dad was showing me love or giving me food I was not allowed to have. I could see her anger but I wouldn't make eye contact with her. I felt like her hate could burn a hole through me if I made eye contact with her. I was feeling a freedom I had never known. I loved having all my brothers and sisters together under one roof, well, except for my older brother, who still chose his moments to be mean when dad was not looking. All this bliss, however, was short-lived. Mother's crazy could not be hidden for very long, and her true colors eventually came shining through like a lighthouse in a closet.

One day, when we were alone, dad had told me how sorry he was for what my stepdad had done. I told him that Richard was kind and never hurt me or anyone else. My Dad was confused and I'm sure he felt used and betrayed. Mother's crazy side showed more and more and she blew up on dad and took us and moved across town. I made sure I memorized dad's phone number and watched closely so I could find my way home if I had to escape. I planned it in my head, and planned to take my little brother and sister with me.

Mother spent several months barhopping, trying to find Mr. Right, her knight who would make her whole. It was as if she had to have a man to complete her. She brought a lot of strangers home and it was not abnormal to wake up to a new man in the house. She even had a couple of nice men who, once her insanity emerged, would be gone.

During this time, the abuse from mother slowed. I don't know if it was because I was older and it was harder to beat the crap out of me, or if she was just so self-consumed that she was more concerned with her dating life than kicking my ass. Although it still happened.

I was still the slave and if I did not have the house perfect, I'd get beat. My brother baked a cake once and did not clean up his mess. Mother came home and asked, "who baked a cake without permission?" My brother, of course, said it was me and she dragged me to the kitchen by my hair, beat the shit out of me, and told me if I ever left the kitchen a mess like that again that she would kill me! And, if I ever used *her* cake mix again, without permission, she would leave me outside naked all night to sleep on the porch.

I kept the house clean, the laundry done, and did all the cooking. Mother was living off welfare and barhopping, so she was gone a lot. It was a nice time for me until something set her off, which could be anything. Some loser she brought home one night said, I was "real cute" and that sent her over the edge. I got my ass kicked for that one and she cut my hair off; I guess so I would not be "cute" anymore. I just never knew what would bring out my mother's wrath!

I remember thinking that I was looking forward to being an adult so I would *never* have to taste blood in my mouth from getting hit by my mother. I hated the taste of blood, the smell of moss, the thought of eating fish or liver. They were all triggers that made me feel like that scared little girl I had always been; I hated that I wasn't brave.

My dad witnessed mother's crazy firsthand and was in shock. When I would go over there for an overnight, we would talk and he came to fully understand that she had manipulated him to get out of Texas. I did get a little brave and said that she was mean to me. I did not fully fill him in on the extent of my abuse but, as I got older, I was getting braver. Not brave enough to tell him everything because I was still afraid of her finding out. But, I was learning that I had a voice and I was trying to learn when it was safe to use it. But for the most part, I still felt weak and hated myself for it.

I went from a terrified, abused kid who wouldn't make eye contact to a rebellious teenager. I was still very obedient and did not talk back to her because it was easier to obey and not talk back than it was to take a beating. But, outside of the home, I smoked, snuck alcohol, and tried drugs. Everything I did helped me forget how sad and miserable I'd become.

Mother was on a crazy rollercoaster ride of emotions. She was exhausting. She would go from being in bed for days to being so happy and excited that she would pull us out of school to go home and clean and make brownies or paint the living room. It was hard to understand and keep up. I was only thirteen, but I knew she was not right in her head. She brought a trail of men home and none of them could make her happy, so I knew it wasn't them. The bottom line was that no one could handle her crazy.

One day, she brought home my second stepdad. I did not see it, he was not wealthy or attractive but at first, he did put up with her insanity. I knew it was doomed to failure and that she would eventually chase him off, too. At first she was happy and that made my life easier, as she beat me less. When it started going bad, the abuse began again. I could not understand how kicking my ass was going to make anything better in her romantic life. She hated me and I could feel that hate. Like she did not even want me to breathe the same air as her and, honestly, I could not wait to be away from her forever. I still had the question I had always wondered and never knew the answer to, why did my mother hate me?

THINGS WE SURVIVE

9
Sharon

Mother was in school during most of my life, searching for something that would make her happy. At this particular time in my life, I believe it was a program to become a respiratory therapist. She made a friend named Sharon and she would come over to do homework and work on projects together. Sharon would sometimes bring her son, Justin, and there were other times I would watch Justin. I really liked her and thought how nice it would be to have her as my stepmother. She was sweet and kind and hugged me. I remember one day she was leaving and "I love you" slipped out of my mouth. I paused and she hugged me closer and said, "I love you, too, sweet girl." I *knew it*! She loved me! It felt good to hear those words. Mother *hated* to see Sharon hug me and show me love.

Dad had been planning a camping trip with me, my little brother Joseph, and my sister Dorothy, and Dorothy and I thought how perfect it would be for Sharon to go with us. So, Dorothy and I set it up, or set them up. Following one of Sharon's visits, I walked Sharon to her car. Once out of mother's earshot, I told Sharon that she should go because dad could not cook and I did not want to starve, and Justin would have fun playing with Joseph. This was not true, as our dad was a great cook, but I was setting up this future couple, or so I hoped and had to come up with something. I told Sharon that dad needed another adult along to keep him company and Justin needed a friend and could play all weekend with my little brother. Dorothy told dad that "poor Sharon" seemed depressed lately and needed to get away and camping would be just what would cheer her up. I fibbed and told dad that Sharon heard we were going and she told me how much she *loved* camping but had not been in such a long time.

I'm not quite sure how it worked, but it did. Sharon went camping with us and we had a fabulous time together. Dad and Sharon started seeing each other and were married soon after.

I was thrilled. Mother was *pissed*. She still wanted my dad but she was too crazy for any man. Mother even told Sharon that she would "allow" her and Dad to date, but when she was ready to get back with him, he would leave her. I remember being embarrassed when she told Sharon this. Sharon and mother were never really friends after that.

Dad had no interest in getting back together with my mother, thank God. Mother was relentless and talked so poorly about Sharon, told so many lies. Mother would not let me watch her son Justin anymore and never missed an opportunity to talk shit about her. Mother would ask me how happy I was that I ruined my dad's life by introducing him to a woman like Sharon. She said that Sharon was sleeping with several men in their Respiratory Therapy class. I am not sure what Mother thought she was accomplishing by being so hateful and telling lies about Sharon. She was acting like a jealous teenage girl who was mad at another woman who was in love with the boy she threw away. She did not want him till she realized someone else did. Juvenile.

Mother made Sharon's life hell at school and the torture was endless. I was so embarrassed that she was my mother. Eventually, she ended up dropping out of school, and I imagine it was an incredibly happy moment for Sharon to know that she did not have to deal with *crazy* anymore.

I was very happy and relieved that Dad and Sharon did not fall victim to her lies and deception. And I am even happier to say that they are still married to this day and even had another baby sister for me, Lindsey. I adored Sharon and I adored being with them. When I was with them, I was allowed to be a kid, I could laugh, smile, and engage in conversations. I was allowed to say, "no, thank you," if offered food I did not like. I was worried that Sharon would not like me being around because of the hell my mother put her through but she loved me unconditionally. When I was with Dad and Sharon, I was happy.

Sharon would do fun things with me. "Just us girls," she would say and I loved it. My sister Dorothy was living with her mom at the time so It was just Sharon and me till my baby sister Lindsey arrived. Sharon was a dream as a mom. We would paint our nails, try out delicious-smelling lotions, and shop till we dropped, things I never did with my mother *ever*. Sharon loved having a girl around and loved to spoil me. I soaked up the love and affection. Mother was pissed at me for introducing them but she was pissed at me for being born, so I no longer cared. I kept my head down and laid low.

Sharon and I had been shopping one day and I saw an outfit I really liked. Sharon noticed me looking at it and asked, "do you like that, Teff?" I did not say anything. I just smiled and Sharon pulled it off the rack, held it up, and said, "I think this will fit perfectly," and put it in the cart. That kind of stuff never happened to me.

I *loved* that outfit and made the mistake of wearing it home. Mother asked me where I got that ugly outfit. When I answered "Sharon," she told me it was a trashy outfit and I was not allowed to wear it in her house. That outfit disappeared the next day while I was at school. I was so sad and embarrassed to tell Sharon. But she was very sweet and told me that when I left, from then on I could wear whatever outfit I was wearing when I came over. I left all the clothes she got me at their house.

Sharon and Dad *never* spoke poorly about my mother in front of me. If they did, I never heard them. They knew she was crazy and had every reason to freely talk shit, but never talked bad about her. As an adult, I am thankful that they taught me that lesson when I was so young. They felt that it was wrong to talk bad about my mother, no matter how crazy she was because she was still my mother and they did not want it to come back later and possibly hurt my feelings.

They were *amazing* examples of how to co-parent. They believed the more people loved their kids, the better their kids were going to be. They felt like there did not have to be negative, nasty exchanges and they could say nice things about exes and come out on top. As an adult, I have always tried to do the same and know how difficult it can be when the other person isn't following the same set of morals and or values.

Because siblings really do love one another, they can talk shit when venting about one another and know they'll eventually work through it. I know, because I have a lot of brothers and sisters and there have been many times some did not speak. Even amongst my own children, because they are all different people and see things differently, disagreements are natural. It's ok for them to get upset and call each other batshit crazy. Just because they have to vent, doesn't mean they don't love each other.

But for one parent to disparage the other in front of the children is so wrong and only hurts the children. And the one doing the shit-talking usually ends up being seen as the asshole by the children. Kids are smart and they know the difference between what they are being told and the truth.

My dad always used to say that, "everything comes out in the wash," and it's so true. I know my mother did some serious shit-talking about a lot of people, especially my parents and stepdad, and she was the only one that looked like a hateful, sad person.

THINGS WE SURVIVE

10

I'm About to Die

When I was in eighth grade, one Saturday morning I was trying to hurry and finish my chores so I could escape the house before mother got back from the library. I was folding laundry on the couch in the living room and the front door came crashing open, hitting the wall and rattling, the whole apartment. I jumped and saw her standing in the doorway. She looked like Satan. She was shaking in anger and, through clenched teeth said, "*get upstairs!*" Without question, I stopped what I was doing and went to the top of the stairs. I did not go into any of the bedrooms; I learned to not assume anything with her. So there I stood at the top of the stairs, waiting for Satan. I knew I was gonna get beat and did not know why, but it was gonna happen and there was nothing I could do to stop it.

Mother came upstairs and through clenched teeth said, *"Take. Off. All. Your. Clothes!"* I did as I was told and stripped down to my bra and panties. She was just standing there watching every move I made as she was shaking, seething with anger and hatred, she looked more evil than I had ever seen her and I was terrified!!! So, I'm standing there at the top of the stairs with nothing but my bra and panties on and there was silence. I glanced up with just my eyes and she said through clenched teeth, "*I said, take off everything!!!*"

I did as I was told and took off the bra and panties and stood there naked, waiting, feeling scared and humiliated. When I glanced up at her to see if she was still standing there, she came out of her room and said, "*get in the car!*" Completely confused, I asked her the first question *ever*, which was, "Naked?" I wanted to be sure that she wanted me to take my naked ass outside to the car where people could see me. She got right up in my face, nose to nose, and through her clenched teeth that I thought were sure to break at any moment under the pressure, said to me, "do you really think anyone wants to see your disgusting body? You're so fucking ugly, no one wants to see you naked, but here," she handed me a small bath towel. And by small, I mean small, almost the size of a bath towel that a child would use.

I started wrapping this tiny towel around me but was apparently not moving fast enough for her and she shoved me down the stairs. The berating and pushing continued all the way out to the car. "How can I be so clumsy, I must be retarded, I think I'm better than everyone." She then threatened to shave the hair off my head since I thought I was so pretty, which I did not. However, she had me convinced I was the ugliest girl in the world. Thanks to her, I had no self-confidence!

So I took my naked ass, with the tiny bath towel, to the car and as I was getting in the front seat as instructed, I saw my baby brother in the back. Looking at me, he asked, confused "where are your clothes?" I told him mother made me take them off. He said, "that is so weird." I told him that "I loved him forever no matter what" and shushed him as mother was getting in the car. I was convinced that this was the moment. She had finally snapped and was about to kill me.

I knew in my heart that I was about to die but I was not afraid of dying. There was almost a peace that I felt by the thought of dying, I just did not want it to hurt. I was a thirteen-year-old girl who had no self-esteem, so I was more afraid of my naked body being found, like an animal on the side of the road. I wondered how long I would be out there naked before someone found me and how many people would see me naked. I was also terrified that animals would eat my dead body.

But I think I was mostly afraid of what would happen to my baby brother in the back seat. Would she have to kill him, too, if he witnessed it? God, please don't let him see my murder.

Mother was enraged at who knows what, but she kept saying, how pathetic I was, how much she hated me, how I destroyed her life. She was screaming all this at me at the top of her lungs as she kept punching me in my face, head, and side. I was leaning up against the door as far as I could to try to avoid the blows. My ear was ringing and I could feel my eye swelling shut and felt the blood gushing from my eyebrow and head.

My baby brother was crying and had gotten on the floor behind my seat and reached around the side of the front seat to touch my arm. He was begging mother to stop but she just kept punching. I shushed him and told him I loved him and told him to close his eyes and promise to not open them until he got home. Mother was screaming that I needed to stop talking to him and to not say that I loved him, saying that I was no longer his sister. She said I was dead to them! But I kept trying to comfort him by shushing him and telling him I did love him no matter what she said, to never forget. I figured if she was about to kill me, I was going to disobey her and stand up to her for the first time in my life.

This is how I was going to die, at the hands of my own mother. I felt like I was losing consciousness. I knew I was bleeding from my head and left eye, which seemed to take the brunt of the beating. Blood was all down my face and soaking the tiny bath towel. My lip felt fat and the taste of blood in my mouth pissed me off, the last thing I'm ever gonna taste is blood.

Then, suddenly, she took an unexpected turn and there was a glimmer of hope. Was she driving me to my dad's? I wanted to scream at her what I thought of her and how sick she was, but I wanted to get to dad's alive and did not want to piss her off to the point that she took me up to the mountains and finished me off.

My baby brother was still holding my arm tight. I leaned down to kiss his hand and said, "I love you forever," as we pulled up in front of dad's house. I reached for the door handle and as I exited the car of Satan, she ripped the tiny, blood-soaked bath towel from my hands and told me, "have a nice life, bitch!!" Despite my battered bleeding body, I felt happiness and freedom as I ran my naked, broken body up to my dad's front door and felt only *relief*.

So, it was not the middle of the night, it was a Saturday morning and people were outside, mowing their yards, playing football in the street, riding bikes, and here I was, bleeding from my face and head, running naked from the car to my dad's door. My stepmom Sharon saw me coming through the front window. She saw me naked and bleeding, and grabbed an afghan from the couch and started heading for the door. Dad was clueless and did not see what was coming. He just heard me pounding on the door and opened it and was shocked, as my stepmom covered me with the blanket and took me straight to the bathroom to clean me up.

I feel so blessed to have such a wonderful stepmother that never questioned taking me in. She patched me up and took me shopping for clothes and everything else I needed. It was hard at first because I was not used to being told, "whatever you need, just ask." She was an amazing mother and never treated me like a stepchild. She would introduce me as her daughter, not her stepdaughter. The only steps in our home were the ones that led to the front door.

Those first few weeks with my dad and stepmom were an awkward adjustment period. I felt love and safety, but I kept having nightmares that mother would come and make me go back. There was no legal documentation that my dad was my legal dad. The name on my birth certificate for my father was not his name, it was my mother's husband's name. Then, when she married Richard, he adopted all her children. So we were in constant fear that she would someday demand that I return. I think that was the only reason my dad did not call the police the day my mother dumped me off on his doorstep, bloody and naked.

Those first few months were a *huge* change for me. We were a family. My stepmom cooked dinner every night and we ate together as a family. There were no strange men in the house every night, there was no daily yelling or hitting. I *loved* my new life. As wonderful as life had become, I was still haunted by the questions, why did my mother hate me? Why did she hate me enough to abuse me the way she did? Was I that bad as a child? Knowing I never talked back, I always did as I was told, I did all the chores, but yet, she still hated me. I knew at this point in my life that my childhood was *not* a normal one and my mother was the opposite of normal. I often wondered if she knew what happened in that bathroom.

Did she know or see what my grandfather did to me and my sister? Did she hate me because she knew what I had done, that I failed to protect my sister? Sometimes, looking in the mirror, I can see the scars on my face from her and wonder how a mother could do that to her own daughter.

Now in the eighth grade, I wasn't the best kid during the first few years with my dad. I was good at home and did not talk back or cause trouble but my bad behavior was escalating outside the home. We had moved to Fresno and I was struggling with new schools, new friends, and had begun smoking, drinking, and experimenting with new drugs.

11

Harold

I met the love of my life in high school and *loved* being with him. Although initially, I thought he was rude and annoying and he thought I was a snob. We fought and told each other off and ended up being friends. The more time I spent with Harold, the more I liked him. I did not know he was interested in me and thought he only looked at me as a friend. We were best friends and told each other everything. We would have these deep discussions and talk about what we wanted in life, places we wanted to go, past mistakes, things we regretted, lies we had told, and secrets we kept.

One night, we were at a park we liked to go to where we would spend hours talking, smoking, drinking, and being away from people. He asked me what happened with my mother. I don't know what came over me, but I told him everything she ever did to me. I found the courage to tell him about what I had been through not only with my mother but I told him what my grandfather did to me and my sister. He hugged me tight and cried with me as I shared all the horrible things I had survived. Not being one to cry in front of others or show any signs of weakness, with Harold I felt safe to open up, talk, be myself, and together, we cried.

I remember falling in love with him that night. Having developed a protective, hardened exterior that kept people at a distance, with Harold I was sobbing and spilling my heart out and he held me and cried with me. We were two kids that had been through terrible things that ended up best friends. He and his brother were adopted but before being adopted by a wonderful couple, he had a rough childhood. We grew closer every day and one night, I told him that I loved him as more than my best friend. I was pleasantly surprised when he confessed that he was in love with me, too. We spent a couple of months sneaking out to be together, spending as much time as possible with each other. Young love is so crazy and so pure, and so confusing.

Harold's ex-girlfriend had called him one day claiming to be pregnant. It was a terrible time for me because I was totally in love with Harold and I did not want to lose him, he was not only my boyfriend, but my best friend. I knew his ex-girlfriend and knew she had pretended to be pregnant before to keep a boyfriend. Teenage girls can be horrible. He was confused and wanted to do right by her and his child. At the time, I was devastated, but now I understand his desire to be there for his child. Having been adopted, for him it was something he *had* to do. When they got back together, I found myself heartbroken, angry, and, once again, alone!

After he left, I spent the first couple of months sad and depressed, So depressed that I felt like throwing up every day. I heard from friends that Harold found out that his girlfriend had, in fact, lied about being pregnant and they had broken up. One night,

Harold had been out drinking and did something stupid and was arrested. All I could think was well, I tried to warn you but you wouldn't listen.

Trying to get my life back to some semblance of normalcy, it had been about three months and I realized I had missed a period, maybe two. Oh, God, what the hell am I going to do? I was sixteen and he was eighteen when I found out I was pregnant. Considering what Harold had just been through, how was I going to tell him that I really *was* pregnant? Should I even tell him? Harold was now in jail and had been sentenced to eight years for his stupidity. I was still hurt and angry and did not want to show him that he had hurt me. Kinda like when my mom would hurt me but I wouldn't give her the satisfaction of crying.

When I was about six months pregnant, I decided I had to tell him about the baby, so I went to the jail with my pregnancy test results and my little baby bump. I told him that I was pregnant and he did not believe me, which broke my heart all over again. As I cried, I held up the pregnancy test results paperwork so he could read it through the glass separating us. When he realized I was being truthful, his eyes welled up with tears. I could not take seeing him cry. I was still so in love with him and so angry, I just wanted to yell at him, but knew I had to stay strong for me and this baby. No more words were spoken. I got up and left and did not look back at this man, this boy I loved with everything in me.

THINGS WE SURVIVE

12

Savannah

On Christmas day, I delivered a beautiful baby girl who weighed five pounds and was perfect. I named her Savannah, after a movie Harold and I had watched. I was sad her daddy wasn't there to see this sweet baby. I often wondered, would he be in jail if he hadn't been taken away from us.

I remember telling my parents that I was pregnant and being terrified. I was hiding the bad side of me and playing the perfect child so my parents would love me and wouldn't send me back to my mother. Yet, like always, they were nothing but loving and supportive, telling me that it was a baby and a baby is a blessing no matter how old its mamma is. My dad had always been there to love me and support me unconditionally and my stepmom was just as awesome. I'm not sure why I was scared to tell them or scared about their reactions; they epitomize *unconditional* love. They are my template for loving parents. I think deep down I knew they would still love me but I did not want to disappoint them since they had been my dream come true as parents.

They had my sister Lindsey, who was just two years old when I told them I was pregnant, so they had their hands full anyway but they were wonderful and embraced being grandparents at their young age. They never made me feel like I was a terrible person for getting pregnant at sixteen. I was not the bad girl my mother had always told me I was. They told me that I made some hard choices but they were proud of me for handling it all and never giving up and getting my high school diploma.

My dad was my labor coach and was there in the delivery room to see his first baby have her first baby. It was such a blessing for him, I'm sure, since he was denied that with me. I remember him holding my daughter and seeing the look of *pure love* in his eyes. I have always remembered that look and imagined that was the way he would have looked at me had he been given the opportunity to have seen me only moments old. Now, looking back, I guess that is the way he has really always looked at me. He may not have always loved the decisions I have made, but it has never changed the way he loves me. I was truly blessed when it came to the dad department.

When Dad left that night, it was just me and my precious baby in the room. It was the wildest Christmas I had ever had and I had the greatest Christmas gift ever. Here I was a *mom*; I was seventeen years old and a baby that had just had a baby. My beautiful Savannah was looking up at me as I cradled her tiny five-pound body in my arms and I promised her that I would never hurt her, that I would never hate her, that I would do my best to always keep her safe, and mostly that I would love her *forever*.

Harold wrote, expressing how grateful he would be if I could find it in my heart to forgive him and if I would call and let him know when the baby was born. He sent me a phone number to the prison and said to give them his name and tell them I had a baby and needed to get word to him. So the day after I had my precious baby, I called the number Harold gave me and told the person who answered that I just had a baby and the father was an inmate there. The man asked me for the inmate's name and put me on hold.

After about a ten-minute wait, Harold came on the line. I was shocked. I did not expect to be talking to this man I was still in love with. I thought that he would just be told that his child was born. But here he was, that voice I missed, the voice of the man I loved. He said "Hello." I asked, "Harold?" He returned with, "Steph?" There was an awkward pause and I was annoyed. I said, "ya, it's Steph. I had the baby yesterday." Another awkward pause, and then he asked, "is it a boy?" That annoyed me even more. I had carried this baby, felt her grow inside of me, was alone without him through every step of the way and he asked if *she* was a boy. I said, "no she's a girl." I'm sure I sounded as annoyed as I felt. I ran down her vitals, weight, length, and time of birth, while holding back the emotions that were flooding through my broken heart.

There was so much left unsaid. I wanted to tell him I still loved him with everything in me, I wanted to ask him to come home to *us* but I could not. I hesitated, sounding annoyed, and he obviously sensed my anger, which I'm sure added to his fear of saying what he wanted to say. So rather than have a call filled with joy, it was awkward and painful. Then, when he said he needed to go, I became annoyed again, not realizing that he was on a time limit being in prison. So sounding like a smart ass I'm sure, I said, "well, ok, bye!"

Looking back, knowing what I know now, I wish I had been a little more patient, a little more understanding about his situation and inability to have opened up and talked to me in that setting. I was just a sad, angry, hormonal seventeen-year-old with a newborn baby girl that was still hurt and wishing things were different. I had no idea that Harold still loved me the way I still loved him. He later told me that he had regret for leaving me and going back to his ex. He knew within a month of going back to her that he had made a bad choice. He, too, wished that he could have gone back and made a different choice, that he never stopped loving me. Had I only known then, I would have made different choices also. But we did not know.

My sister called me the day after Savannah was born and I could hear Mother's voice in the background, it made me cringe. My sister sounded disappointed, saying, "well, if you're home, I take it that you did not have the baby." This was back in the day when you did not know what you were having till the baby arrived. Mother heard what my sister asked and in her most annoying, *smarter than everyone tone* said, "I told you she wouldn't have had the baby on Christmas!" So I *loved* being able to respond with, "well, tell Ms. smarter than everyone that she is wrong—I had the baby yesterday and *she* is perfect."

My sister squealed and said, "she had the baby; it's a girl." We chatted about the stats, five pounds, nineteen inches long, and perfect. She was giddy and when she heard Savannah's sweet little newborn "I'm hungry" cry, she almost exploded. She asked mother, "can we go see her?" Of course, I heard mother say "No" and "that kid is never gonna call me grandma." All I could think was, "Well, you're right, because she is never gonna know you and she has a grandma and her name is Sharon."

And, almost on cue, my loving mom Sharon walked in, smiled, and asked, "you good, Teff? Need anything?" She leaned down and kissed my newborn baby on the forehead and said, "Grandma loves you, baby girl." I felt so blessed that I had my mom, Sharon, and that she loved me unconditionally and it did not matter that I was only seventeen with a newborn living under her roof. There was *no* judgement, *no* disappointment, just a momma's love.

When Savannah was just a couple of months old, I was happy to be able to see my sister again. I had gone to Jeffi's to see her but tried to plan it for when mother would not be there. I did not want to see her and I did not want her to see my precious baby. I was also afraid that she would make a shitty comment about Savannah and I would have to blow up on her.

I was happy that mother was not there but I was sad my baby brother had been shipped to his dad's in Texas. I was happy to think that Jay wasn't there to have to be forced to live with this psychotic woman that happened to give birth to us. I love the idea of him being with my first dad. I was not sure why she shipped him off, other than she probably could not handle a child she could not manipulate. Jason saw her rage; he saw her almost kill me. Mother tried to tell him I did not love him and I told him otherwise the night she beat me almost to death. I told him I loved him as she was pummeling my face and it was not stopping me from making sure he knew I loved him. He was a very strong-willed child and he drove mother crazy. She did not like people that could think for themselves and people that would say, "no, it did not happen that way!"

I went to visit Jeffi a couple of times a month, so I did run into mother occasionally. I was shocked that my mother actually acted like nothing had ever happened and she had not abused me all my life till she dumped me off at my dad's. I kept my distance for my own mental health but I loved being a part of my sister's life again. We had been through so much together.

My older brother also seemed to have forgotten being such an asshole to me when I was young. He even acted like mother was the only problem growing up. I was extremely apprehensive of his sudden interest in being a caring brother to me as much as I was about my mother's behavior. She suddenly wanted to be my mom but I had a mom and her name was Sharon. This other woman was my *mother*, the woman that hated me and wished I was never born.

My goal at that point was to be the best mom I could be to this precious baby. I finished school through adult education so I would have a high school diploma. I ended up moving in with a friend of mine who also had a baby as a teenager. She was getting married and she and her husband had a studio apartment they rented to me. It was the first time in my life that I was in control. I had my own place, my own child, my own new life. I could buy the groceries I *wanted*. Other than being a good mom, I'd not yet determined what I wanted to do next with my life.

I so loved being a mom and I really loved my little Savannah. She was such a good baby, thank God. She slept through the night and did everything with a little smile on her beautiful face. I would often look at her and wonder how my mother could have gone through all this with me yet hate me so much. Which begged the question, did she go through all this with me, was she actually present for me as a baby, or did she leave me in my crib to cry?

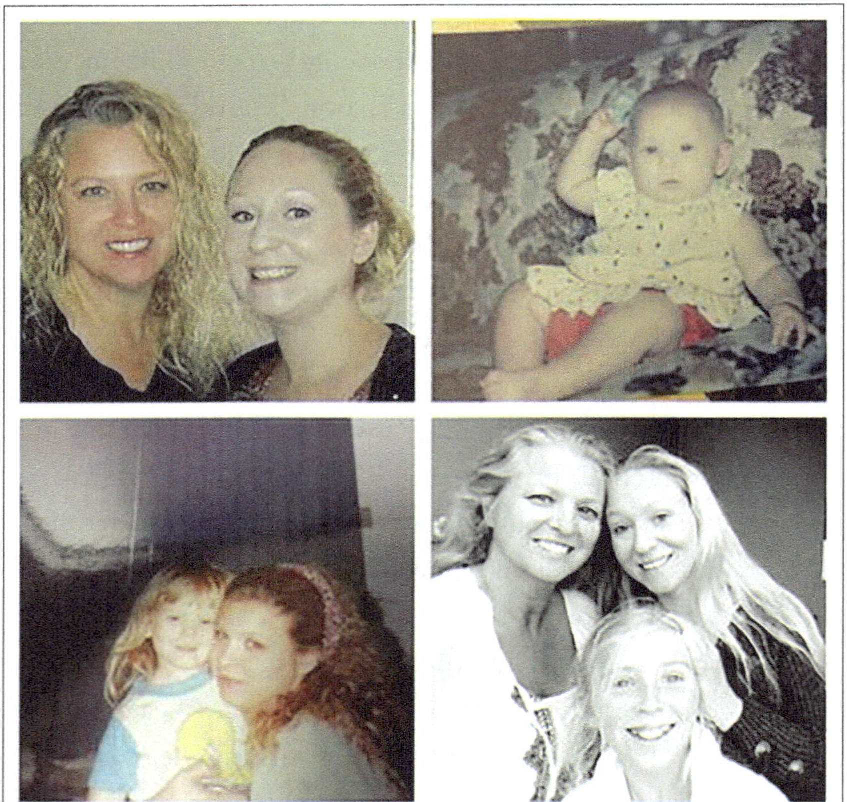

13

Jellybean

When I was eighteen, I met a man who I thought was wonderful. We began to date and he seemed to adore my daughter. I was very protective of my daughter and *loved* that we had a happy little family, no abuse, no hate, just love and laughs. But I missed Harold and had not heard from him. I was convinced that he was just not interested in me or his daughter.

So when Kenny came along and seemed to adore my daughter, I slowly let him become a part of our lives. We started talking and he told me he also had a daughter, but never saw her. He said her mother kept her from him, which made me feel bad for him. We dated briefly and ended up getting married. His family welcomed me into their family and they adored my daughter.

Less than a year later, I had my second child, Joan. She was a preemie and so tiny, I called her my Jellybean. Her sister Savannah was Pumpkin, but she was too tiny to be a pumpkin, so she was my Jellybean. I thought her sister was tiny at five pounds, but she was super tiny at four pounds. She was in a hospital in the NICU an hour away, since that was the closest NICU, not like now where there is a NICU in almost every hospital.

Unlike when my first daughter was born, I did not get that alone time with Joan, as she was whisked away to the NICU. It was a couple hours before I first saw her and they were the longest two hours of my life. I remember having to scrub and gown up before even being allowed to go see my baby. When I first saw her, I almost passed out, as she was so tiny. There were tubes going in and out of her tiny little body, a machine breathing for her, and she was in an incubator. The nurses were wonderful and had a rocking chair next to her incubator so I could sit and visit with my baby. So, I reached in and touched her little hand and made her the same promise I had made to her sister, *that I would never hurt her, that I would never hate her, that I would do my best to always keep her safe, and mostly that I would love her **forever**.* I could not stop crying. There were so many whys haunting my thoughts. Why had I failed her? Why had my body gone into labor so early? Why was my baby so compromised? Why was I alone? Why wasn't my husband here? I was nineteen years old, terrified, and asking only *why?*

One of the nurses came over and put her arm around me to comfort me. She gave me tissues and asked if I wanted to know what all the machines were doing. I said yes, and she lovingly and clearly explained everything to me in a way I could understand. I was terrified but calm, knowing that that woman was taking care of my baby. I stayed in the NICU till they asked me to go lay down in my room. They always had the NICU clear of parents when they did AM and PM rounds to review the babies' conditions with the oncoming care team.

I was in the hospital for two days after having my little Jellybean. My blood pressure was stabilized, so they said I could go home, but leaving that hospital without my daughter was one of the hardest things I'd ever been asked to do. Regardless of living an hour away, I went to see her every day. While at the hospital, my sister-in-law was wonderful and watched my oldest daughter.

Bringing home my tiny baby on my original due date was one of the happiest days of my life. This little girl was a fighter and I knew how strong and special she must be for God to have allowed her to come home to her family. I felt like having my girls together was the greatest blessing I had ever been given. They were the best little girls and I showered them with all my love.

Supporting my girls became a constant stress as my husband could not seem to keep a job. My little Jellybean was thriving and growing like a weed. She *loved* being in her little papoose and staring up at me as I would be cleaning the house and singing to her. She would laugh and adored when her big sister was around, and my sweet Savannah was the best big sister. I felt so blessed with my sweet girls, which made me sad for my husband as he was being denied the same opportunity with his oldest daughter, Krystal. So I pushed him to reach out to her mother and determine what was necessary to be a part of her life.

My husband finally reached out to his daughter's mother and she agreed to let Kenny and I come see Krystal. I was excited to meet her, but Kenny seemed nervous. I remember pulling up in front of her house and she was standing at the door looking excited and so sweet.

We went into the house and visited, and I met Krystal and her mom. I remember trying to figure out how we both had loved the same man as she and I were polar opposites. I was impressed with how sweet, smart, and affectionate Krystal was. It came as no surprise that she asked her mom right away when she could spend the night with dad.

The girls hit it off immediately. Savannah *loved* having a big sister and Krystal was wonderful with both girls. I loved all three of my girls.

14

The Fall of Kenny

My husband continued to spend more time away from home, doing what I had no idea but he wasn't bringing home a paycheck. We struggled to pay the bills and keep the babies fed. Kenny began drinking a lot and I suspected he was doing drugs as well, but it would start a fight every time I questioned him. I think he may have been selling weed at the time or stealing to make rent. I was in constant fear that the cops would show up, find weed, and take my babies. I found a bag in my car over the visor once and when I asked him about it, he blamed it on my brother. At the time, weed was illegal and I was no drug dealer, but the large bag that dropped from my visor was definitely a *huge* drug charge.

Things were easier for me and the girls when he was gone and I suspected he might be seeing another woman, but I had no proof. There was less stress and no arguing; I even think he sensed I was not happy and would be OK if he just left. So, he came home one day and said he was enlisting in the Navy. I was beyond shocked but pleased, because that was a job he could not just quit like he had every other job.

He started drinking something he called a cleanse every day, he apparently thought I was an idiot. I asked what he had to cleanse out of his system and he said nothing, that it was just a precaution since he was around people that smoked weed. Now I'm not sure who would have bought that bullshit, but I certainly did not and I hated to be lied to, but I was going to let it slide since this career choice was going to be a good thing for our family.

Kenny went to boot camp and graduated and we were stationed in the bay area. Our housing was on the Oakland Army Base (OAB). It was amazing to have the security of knowing that I wouldn't be evicted for not making rent. For my constantly stressed heart, it was a relief. My husband was going to have a job I knew he could not quit for at least four years and we had a home with no electric or gas bills. It was heaven.

Shortly after we settled in Oakland, Operation Desert Storm launched and my husband was deployed to the Persian Gulf. It was an amazing time with the girls and settling in to the comfort of not worrying, until I went to the commissary to get groceries and my bank card was declined.

He was paid once a month, so I planned shopping and meals on a month-to-month basis. This was quite the mission to ensure we had enough food to last the entire month. So there I stood, two carts full of groceries to last a month, two little girls, and a declined card. I was embarrassed and ashamed. I apologized, left all the groceries, and went to the bank to find out what the problem was. Well, the problem was that my husband had pulled all of his paycheck out and the account had twenty-three dollars in it. I was *pissed* and suddenly scared, I could not call him and ask what the hell, as he was on a ship in the middle of the ocean.

When I got home, the base chaplain was at my door. He introduced himself and I shook his hand. He said he had gotten a call from the cashier at the commissary after I left. She is a Navy wife also and she was concerned when I left. She knew I had no money and obviously no groceries. He went down to the commissary and paid for my groceries. I was overwhelmed and embarrassed. He said that we were an OAB family and we all looked out for each other. I told him I could pay him back as soon as I figured out what happened, even though I knew what happened, my loser husband took his paycheck out before I could use the money for our family.

The chaplain said that there was no need to pay it back but when I was able, I could make a donation to the emergency fund that helped OAB families. I tried not to, but I cried as I helped this kind man unload the month's worth of groceries and thanked him. He asked if he could pray with me before he left. We knelt in prayer and I felt the kindness this man had in his heart. He hugged me and the girls when he left and I knelt in prayer again and thanked God for the blessing of the OAB Family Emergency Fund. Then I was *pissed*. How the hell could my husband take all the money out of our account and not leave enough for me to feed our kids? I spent the next couple of weeks trying to figure out what to do if the asshole I was married to pulled all the money out of our account again.

I heard a woman at the playground saying that another neighbor of ours was looking for a babysitter for her two boys. I asked if she could let the woman know I'd be interested. I was home all day and it would give me some money to buy groceries. It worked out perfectly and I definitely needed it when the next payday came and the asshole took out all his money again. I managed to keep food on the table and I was very creative in making our meals stretch.

15

Buster

During this deployment, I found out that I was pregnant again. I *knew* that I needed to find a way to be self-sufficient. I was twenty-two and having another child with a man that I had no future with. I knew in my heart that my husband was not going to be around forever and that did not really bother me. He was not very nice, he lied to me a lot and was very quick to pick a fight with me.

When he finally called me from the United Arab Emirates (UAE), I told him I was pregnant and he seemed annoyed, he definitely was not happy about it. As if I got myself pregnant! I asked him why he kept pulling his paychecks out every payday. He had some stupid lie he told about it being a mistake and eventually it would all be fixed and back in the account. I knew he was full of shit so I told him about the base chaplain and how he paid for the groceries. He seemed a little nervous and said I should not have let him do that and I better not talk bad about him to the base chaplain or anyone.

Here he was on the other side of the world, withholding money and now picking a fight.

He continued pulling all but two hundred dollars out of the account each payday. I was unsure how he thought fifty dollars per week was enough to feed the kids, but he obviously did not care. The greater question was, what was he doing with it? He was on a ship in the middle of the ocean!

The girls were excited about the baby. Savannah wanted a baby brother and Joan wanted a baby sister. Joan said, well, maybe mommy can have both. Thank God, that wish of hers did not come true. I just wanted a healthy baby that did not need to be in the NICU like my little Joan. This time, I was sick every day, which made me afraid that it would happen again. It was a very tough pregnancy, but I was happy to be in this little base community where the kids had friends, we attended the base church, and I served where I could. I made enough at my job to keep food on the table and I loved my little world.

When my husband got home, my life completely changed. He was angry, mean, and much worse than before he deployed. He became obsessed with getting out of the military and this became a constant battle between us. Realizing I had extra money from my babysitting job, he began finding ways to take that as well. Something always hurt, his back, his knee, his head ached and we spent hours and hours at the emergency rooms in every town in our area. He was drug-seeking and there was nothing I could say to dissuade him. He would sleep constantly and be pissed if the girls woke him up. He started spending a lot of time away from home and would bring "friends" home to party. We fought a lot. It was a horrible time in my life and I wanted him to be deployed again. Life was better when he was gone.

I started looking into possible careers that would support me and my babies. I had limited resources but I knew I had to be able to support my kids on my own because my husband was not grasping the family concept.

I made it eight months into my pregnancy and was beyond thrilled to welcome a son, Buster. Even though he was five weeks early, he was a healthy baby who could breathe on his own and was my biggest baby at seven pounds. He was a difficult baby, but I adored my son. I hoped having a son would make my husband happy, since nothing else did. But I was wrong. He continued taking my money as well as pulling out his paychecks before I was able to access them. All the while insisting I made enough to still buy groceries and that I should stop complaining!

When my son was about one, my husband got deployed for a short tour and I was thrilled with the peace of him being gone. I was not feeling well and had some bad stomach pains just before he left, but I did not want to tell him because he would use it as an excuse to *not* go. He left and about two weeks later, I could not take the pain anymore. I had a neighbor watch the kids and went to the Navy hospital ER. After a few hours, blood tests, and ultrasounds, a doctor came in and told me I had Pelvic Inflammatory Disease (PID), a sexually transmitted disease. What? I'm married—that is impossible. I had never been with anyone other than my husband. I laid in that bed feeling humiliated, embarrassed, and ashamed. The doctor was kind and told me I just needed a shot, antibiotics, and some pain medication. I would have to hide the pills or my husband would take them.

When he returned, I was pissed and told him what had happened and he blew up, asking who had I been sleeping with. I told him he *knew* it was him and that I was over his secrets and lies. That was the first time he hit me! He called me a "slut" and punched me in the face. I laid on the floor with blood in my mouth, wondering how I had gotten there. Again, with the taste of blood in my mouth, but now, I had three babies to protect.

During the days following, I decided that I *had* to go back to school. I had to get myself into a position of control to find a way to support myself and my children. *Knowing* that my husband had cheated, bringing home and sharing his STD was crushing; wondering who he contracted it from was still hurtful. And the fact he was trying to blame it on me just *pissed* me off! He even went as far as to say he went to the doctor and the doctor said he did not have any STDs, so it was *me* cheating. I had not been with anyone else, so I knew he was not only a cheater but also a liar. Just lying in the same bed with him at night made me feel sick. How dare he cheat! How dare he steal from me! How dare he hit me! I was so sad, so embarrassed, and so angry. I wanted to call my dad and tell him everything but I was ashamed. Dad never liked Kenny and did not even attend our wedding. I should have listened to my dad.

My husband finally got what he wanted. After constantly complaining about back pain and a knee injury, he was discharged early from the Navy. We moved back home and the real nightmare began. He never held down a job for long and was constantly high, sleeping around, and picking fights. I did not trust having sex with him out of fear of getting another STD, which caused even more fighting. When I did give in to shut him up, I was left terrified. Knowing I could never get him to change, I found it easier to do my own thing.

THINGS WE SURVIVE

16

Abused Again

I began standing up to him, to the point he'd become so enraged, I knew he was about to hit me, then I would back down. One night, he came home drunk, high, and wanted to have sex. I refused and told him he was drunk and to go sleep it off in the living room or I would. When he refused to leave the bedroom, I sighed loudly and got up, grabbed my pillow, and was heading to the living room when he grabbed me by my ponytail, yanking me back to the bed. He said he wanted to make love to his wife, that he was going to and I could do it the easy way or the hard way. I tried to fight him off but he was stronger than me. I fought hard and was screaming, but he covered my mouth. He seemed to like the fight. I finally stopped fighting him and let him do what he wanted. I cried the whole time. I felt sick. I felt weak. I was mad that I was not able to fight him off.

When he was done, he had the nerve to say, "See how nice that was? I love you," and he finally passed out. I went to take a shower and went to the couch and cried myself to sleep. In the morning, I noticed that I had bad bruises on my arms and wrists and upper lip, so like the abused child I used to be. I covered the bruises with a flannel shirt and makeup, and never talked about it. Unfortunately, that was not the last time he did that. Sometimes I was able to fight him off; sometimes he got what he wanted.

My husband raped me and I did not say anything to anyone. At the time, I did not look at it as clear as I do now. At the time, I did not know it was rape. He was my husband, so that wasn't rape or was it? It felt like I was raped. I just happened to be married to the asshole raping me.

There was fear, shame, and embarrassment that, at the time, I could not understand. If I could talk to my younger self, I would tell myself to not be afraid, I would tell myself to take my babies and go, I will be ok. Save yourself and your children a lot of pain and suffering in the future and *Go Now!* I wished I had listened to what my heart was telling me but, sadly, I did not until it was too late. And that mistake, I will live with until I take my last breath.

I spent the next couple of years being a sad woman who had no control over anything in my life. I loved watching my babies grow into sweet little people. I protected them from the horrors of my husband as best I could but he was harsh. He had a very explosive personality and would snap at the smallest of triggers. One day, my niece, Missy, was over to spend the night. My girls were sick and they were all piled up on the couch in the living room watching a video, covered up with blankets. My husband came home, was angry about something, and went back out. He then came back in, screaming at the girls to get their asses out there and clean up their mess on the patio. They jumped up and went outside as he began hosing off the patio and yelling at them.

Watching through the sliding glass door, I was in the dining room folding laundry at the table when my niece asked what was wrong with him. I said I did not know. It was cold out there, so I wanted to get the girls back inside quickly. At that moment, he raised the hose and squirted the girls, soaking them. It was December and freezing outside!

My niece gasped as I opened the sliding glass door and told the girls to come inside. He was *pissed*! Said they were not done cleaning their mess. I told him they were coming in and getting changed and I would clean up their mess. As we came into the house, I asked my niece if she would run the girls a warm bath, and I told the girls to get in the tub and I would bring them some warm jammies. I went to the girls' room to get their jammies and I peeked in on my son who was asleep on my bed. I turned to leave the bedroom after seeing that my baby was still sleeping and had not been disturbed by his lunatic fathers screaming. I turned around and there he was, obviously enraged.

He grabbed me by my throat and drove me to the bed, right on top of my son. I was trying to get free and off my sleeping child. But he was intent on choking me to death, or so it felt. Just as I thought I was going to pass out, my niece was on his back hitting him and screaming at him to get off me. He got off me and went back to finish hosing off the patio. My niece was crying and asked what was wrong with him. She called her mom, who was my husband's sister, and they came to get her. She obviously did not want to spend the night anymore. She told me that what he did wasn't right and I should leave him.

I was really happy that someone else had seen his violence. I'm not sure what I thought would happen but I did not feel so alone anymore. I told myself there was finally a witness and if he went too far and killed me, then maybe she would come forward and tell what she saw that day. I'm not sure what my niece and her parents discussed when they were driving home but it was never mentioned again. I guess I had hoped she would tell her parents and they would come rescue me from the hell I was living in. But that never happened. It was never talked about. There was a lot that this family did not want to talk about.

Kenny was abusive from that point on, and I never knew what would set him off. I hid every bruise and made excuses for every fat lip. He choked me many times and I was always afraid that he would one day go too far and kill me. One time, he grabbed my hand, squeezed and twisted it backwards, actually breaking several fingers.

I knew I had to get out of this horrible situation. I knew if I stayed with him I was giving my daughters permission to accept that terrible behavior in any potential boyfriend or husband and I was giving my son permission to abuse the women in his life. I did not want that, I did not want them to be OK with abuse.

I saw him do some shady things over the years, illegal things, like insurance fraud. He spent more time trying to get out of work than he actually worked. I lived in fear that his shady shit and drug involvement would someday bring the police to our home and I would be arrested or lose my children because he would have *no problem* letting me take the fall for him. He would not have batted an eye and I knew it. He probably already had a story planned.

17

Starting School

I finally started school, enrolling in a program to be a Dental Assistant. My end goal was to become a hygienist, but I was finally at the beginning of my journey. I was excited, nervous, and so ready to take control of my life. I had never been a good student and was not even able to finish high school, although I did get my GED. Back in the eighties, it was frowned upon to be pregnant in high school and they shipped us "bad influence" girls to adult education. I had always been considered a bad girl by my mother and then by the Fresno Unified School district.

One of my classes was a psychology class. It was such a blessing to learn some things that seemed to fit my life and my mother. I dove into psychology and could not get enough. I learned about bipolar disorder and realized that my mother was actually sick. She had all of the symptoms. It was as if someone wrote the description and symptoms of bipolar disorder for *my mother*. The more I learned, the more I wanted to expand that knowledge.

My psychology class was over but I continued to research bipolar illness. I came to the conclusion that my mother was bipolar. Undiagnosed. And unmedicated. Suddenly, my childhood made sense. Surprisingly, I felt sorry for my mother. I was still pissed that she had treated me so badly and that she had almost beat me to death, but now knew she was sick. I felt like I needed to forgive her. However, I was not ready to allow her close enough to my heart that she could inflict pain. But, I believed for my own peace of mind I had to forgive her, I had to let go of the anger held in my heart towards her.

Don't get me wrong, I did not drive over to mommy's, knock on her door, and throw myself into her loving embrace. For starters, I wasn't *that* ready and she probably would have asked me what the hell I was doing there. I still needed to keep her at a distance but I was going to try to let go of the sadness and hate in my heart for what she did to me. I recognized that I could not be mad at an epileptic for having seizures, so I could not hate my mother for being bipolar. I knew it would be a long road to healing but I also knew I had to be the one to take the first step. I just wasn't sure how or where to begin that healing process.

My baby brother was back from Texas and staying with me and he was as helpful as possible and I *loved* having him around. We decided to buy an airline ticket for his dad, Richard, to come out as a Christmas gift to him and he *loved* the idea. It was a fun Christmas and we enjoyed the time with him. My mother, of course, decided to "drop in," trying to hijack the visit. Luckily, my sister called me in advance and forewarned me that mother was on her way over to surprise us. Her sick mental torture continued. So I told Richard she was on her way, allowing him and Jason to go have lunch elsewhere, giving me time to get rid of mother.

Mother showed up and I asked her, "What the hell are you doing there?" She said, "I just wanted to say hello to Richard. It's been too long; why would I not want to see him and say hello?" I let her know that Richard did not want to see her and that he was already gone. "Why wouldn't he want to see me?" she asked. I was flabbergasted! Was she serious? I was an adult standing in *my* house and still felt like she was trying to intimidate me, but I was *not* going to allow her that power.

I mustered up all my strength and bravery and said, "Richard hates you and rightfully so, you lied about him and to him and tried to ruin his life. But you failed. He's happy and none of us kids hate him; we love him." She was in complete shock. Never in my life had she had so little power over me. She turned and walked out and apparently lied to my sister and said I was rude and mean to her. My thought was, well, the truth hurts so maybe she took it as mean. I felt a strength I had never felt before.

She no longer scared me. I was not afraid of her anymore and she knew it. It was an exciting feeling. I felt sorry for her and realized she was a sad, lonely person. Her bipolar disorder had brought her to this place in her life and she was a sad shell of a woman. Then I felt bad for taking so much pleasure in hurting her as deeply as that apparently had. I had to remember that she was sick, literally sick in her mind.

I have always believed in God and feel like I have always been a good person, and I know there are things in life for which people must repent. Knowing there are things I need to repent for, I now questioned if this was something I should repent for, but I also felt like I was justified in my anger for all the abuse I endured. But maybe that, too, is something I need to repent for, the justifying of my actions. I now have a list of things I've not yet repented for. Considering the many things I've yet to forgive, I hope to die slowly, like freezing to death, giving me time to repent. Maybe someday I will be able to let go of everything; I'll continue to try.

    I finished college and graduated Valedictorian, which was not an easy task. I had three kids and a useless husband. School was one of the hardest things I have ever done but I *knew* I had to do it to be able to support my children. I had a Bachelor of Science degree and was finally proud of myself for the first time in my life.

18

Big Mistake

My husband was realizing that I did not need him, or realized that I was about to be able to have a good job and would probably leave him. Either way, he started planting seeds about leaving California. He told me that he had been doing drugs, shocker, "I already knew that asshole." But his mental manipulation was perfectly honed at this point and he said, "If I am going to be successful in totally staying clean, I'm gonna need to be away from my drug connections here, and I'm really gonna need your love and support." Dumbfounded, I'd been snowed and fully bought into it.

Apparently, I was completely naive as *I wanted to believe* that maybe he was remorseful over everything he had put us through. *I wanted to believe* that maybe he was that wonderful man I believed him to be in the beginning. *I wanted to believe* that it was the drugs that had caused him to change. *I wanted to believe* that I could save him. Insert "eye roll" from the woman who quickly realized believing was not enough to fix what was broken in this man.

To start a new life in Arkansas, we packed up everything we could fit in a U-Haul, my car, and my niece's car and off we went. My husband had a sister there and they raved about how cheap it was to live. After a week in Arkansas, I got a job at a dental office with an awesome dentist who I am still friends with to this day. I loved working in the dental field and was so proud that I alone was able to support my family. My husband was constantly looking for work and never held down a job for more than a week. Here we were again! Kinda like he was in California but now instead of hanging out with his drug buddies, he was hanging out with his new drug connection, his own sister. She was in the next town over with her husband and teenage son, who I will refer to as Todd.

Kenny would hang out there until late into the night and would often call and say, "I'm too tired to drive, I will see you tomorrow." And sometimes he would not even make that call. This was before everyone had a cell phone, so if I got home and no one was there, I would call his sister's and—sure enough, he was there. I did not care if he was by himself, but when he had the kids, it would piss me off. I did not want the kids to miss school. I did not want them to be around his drug use or to think this was acceptable behavior. Regardless of what I did not want, this went on for a couple of years.

I *hated* everything about Arkansas, except my job. The kids and I had some fun together at a lake we liked to go to on weekends, but Kenny was never around. I worked a lot of hours and a lot of overtime to make ends meet, so my time with the kids was precious to me. My husband was back to his previous behavior of not being able to hold down a job, drug seeking at numerous emergency rooms, doing what drugs I did not know and at this point, did not care!

After a couple of miserable years, I was in a car accident. One morning on my way to work after dropping the kids off at school, I was hit by a truck on the passenger side of my car. Thank God, it wasn't the driver's side. The force of the impact and the pouring rain propelled my car into a spin and I was hit a second time. Dazed and unsteady, I tried getting out of my car but was stopped by a woman that explained an ambulance was on the way. Aside from severe whiplash, a concussion, and a fairly decent size knot on my forehead, I wasn't severely injured. I tried to call my husband several times and, of course, there was no answer. I then called his sister and again, no answer. At this point, I was pissed and called my boss to let him know what had happened. Fortunately, he was able to pick me up from the hospital.

That morning, my husband split the second I left with the kids and went to his sister's to get high but they were ignoring my calls. This behavior had become normal, I could never count on him to be there for me or our kids. I hated being in Arkansas away from my family and friends, I felt so alone. It was a very sad and lonely time, but I had my kids and we enjoyed our time together when I was off. They were turning into really cool little people. I felt so blessed to have had them when I was so young. It wasn't always easy, but they were my world and worth every sacrifice.

19

Going Back to Cali

I made a decision that day to get out of Arkansas. My kids hated it. I hated everything about it except my job, which I still loved, and I adored my boss. I received a decent settlement from my accident and told my husband I was leaving and going back to California. At least in California, I'd be around family and away from tornados. Fortunately, we had been in only one, which I survived alone with my children as my loser husband was off somewhere getting high.

I did not put the whole settlement in the bank because I knew my husband would pull it all out. I only deposited one thousand and within two days he had that spent. I asked where it went and he said he owed his buddy some money. I told him that he should have paid his drug dealer with *his* money. He said I was stupid and did not know what I was talking about. I was *enraged* but left it alone. I knew what was going on and he just thought I was stupid. I was happy I had withheld the rest of my settlement. I needed that money to escape

Arkansas. I left the money in my locker at work where I knew it was safe from the lying drug addict to whom I was married.

My boss took it hard that I was leaving but understood. He wanted me to come back to train his new lead Registered Dental Assistant (RDA) after I settled in. So he arranged his two-week vacation starting the week I left. He and his wife bought a round trip ticket for me to return for a week and train the new head RDA.

We packed up and left for California, me, my kids, my niece LeeAnne, and my loser husband. It was my Jellybean's birthday and she was so thrilled. I felt bad that we weren't having a party, but she said that going home was as good as any party. She rode with me all the way to California with my son. Savannah rode with my niece and the loser drove the truck. It was a long two days but the moment I saw the Pismo Beach City Limits sign, I cried. I was so happy to be home. I had never lived on the beach, but I had been there for trips in the summer. I remember thinking people that lived there were soooooo lucky.

My in-laws lived in Pismo, so that is where we started. The next morning, we went in search of a place to live and got lucky. We found a three-bedroom in Shell Beach that was very reasonably priced, unusual for the area, but I believed this is where God wanted us.

I had prepared a resume while still in Arkansas and had several copies on hand. On our second day back on the central coast, I went to find a job. I prayed I would be as lucky as I was in Arkansas with my last boss. On day four, I found a job. Everything went so smooth and I knew this was where God wanted me. Luckily, I had the money from my settlement and was able to secure the house and pay two month's rent up front. I opened my own checking account, keeping my money safe from the drug addict who had a bank card attached to our joint account. I had all the utilities turned on for the new house, registered the kids for school, and moved into our little home.

While picking up groceries with my husband the day before I left to fly back to Arkansas, he said he needed money for the week, since I was going to be gone. I asked, "for what?" I'd already made sure the car was full of gas and there were groceries in the cupboards. I even bought him a carton of his cigarettes. So, for the next six days while I was gone, he would be fine. This pissed him off and he started screaming at me about everything. He said fine, that he just wouldn't be there when I returned. Of course, this caught me off-guard and freaked me out. I knew he wouldn't actually take the kids but the thought of coming home to an empty house terrified me. So I then asked him how much he needed and why. He said, "at least a thousand." *What in the hell would he need a thousand dollars for?* I was going to be gone for six days, not six weeks.

I lied to him for the first time. I don't lie well, and I was afraid he was going to see right through me, but I said, "You're hilarious, I don't have a thousand dollars!" He argued with me, asking what the hell I was spending our money on. I corrected him and said, "*my money,*" and I reiterated to him the expenses I had just covered to move back to California, two month's rent, moving expenses, and utilities. There was an awkward moment of silence, then he asked how much I had. Five hundred, I said. He asked for my bank card so he could take money out, but I did not want to give him my card. Then he would know I was lying about my balance. So I said no, that I needed it while I was in Arkansas. But we stopped on the way home and I pulled out two hundred dollars and gave it to him. He was not happy and said, "I thought you said we had five hundred dollars?" I said I was not giving him everything to go blow on drugs, I needed some till my first payday. He, of course, acted insulted and started yelling at me again, that I was a bad wife and that I was hiding *our* money. It was ridiculous but I did not argue, I just took the verbal lashing and bit my tongue so I wouldn't blow up and end up getting hit.

    I went back to Arkansas for a week and the only reason I was not worried about the kids was because my niece LeeAnne was there. I knew that even if he did not cook dinner or he disappeared, my niece would be there to take care of my children. It was a fun week and I was spoiled by my boss and his wife. I stayed at their home, and he and I would go to the office in the morning and at night, his wife Laura would have wonderful things planned. She called it the "pamper package" for coming back and helping them. We had amazing meals at lovely restaurants, hour-long full body massages, and some wonderful gifts in my room every night, including cozy jammies for me. I had never been treated so nice. It was a wonderful week and I knew I would miss them and forever treasure our time together. I fully trained the woman taking my place and wrote her a note to find the following Monday, asking her to please take care of the Blacks for me, and that if she took care of them, they would be wonderful to her. I flew home to California to start my next journey.

20
Todd

I came home to find my husband high. Of course, he was always high. I had been home about six weeks when my husband said that his sister from Arkansas was coming out for a visit and bringing her son, Todd. I was not thrilled but what could I do? I was working a lot of hours and the kids were in school. The next day was a Saturday and my husband was off somewhere, probably getting high. My sweet little Jellybean came to me, crying. She told me through her sobs that "she did not want Todd to come here." I asked her "why" and got a sick feeling in my stomach. She was so brave and told me that "Todd had molested her in Arkansas." Wait, what? I can't possibly be hearing this correctly. My heart hurt so bad, I *knew* what my baby girl had endured. I did not know details yet but I knew the terror, the pain, the fear. I did not know what else to do other than what I had hoped my mother had done. I took her into my arms and told her that she was so incredibly brave for telling me and I would make sure that Todd did not *ever* come here again.

Kenny came home and I told him what our daughter had told me. He did not say anything. I thought he would be enraged. I wanted him to go kill that little pervert. How was he not as devastated as I was? I told him we needed to call the police and file a report. He said *no*, that he would handle it and he left. *No?* I must stand up for my daughter. I have to make sure he doesn't do this again. My heart was so broken that I'd failed my sweet little Jellybean. God, I hated myself for not seeing her pain. How could I have not seen this? God, please help me help my baby girl.

I called the police and went down to the police station and my amazing strong, brave, baby girl told her story, something I was never brave enough to do. I had so much sadness in my heart and yet I was so incredibly proud of her bravery. She was in fourth grade and showed more bravery in that moment than I could ever have at that age. She was my *hero*.

I was so disappointed in my husband for how he handled that situation. Yes, he made sure that Todd wouldn't come to our house, but he was mad at *me* for calling the police and filing a report. He said we should have handled it within the family. One family member even told my daughter that what Todd had done wasn't molestation but rather the curiosity of kids. All I could think was how sick these people were. I was the *only* family member that stood up for my daughter and I was the one everyone was pissed at. No one but me believed her and it pissed me off. I did not care if they never spoke to me again. I did the right thing in protecting my baby. I was alone in my fight to protect my baby girl, but I was OK with that. She was my top priority.

I was even more disappointed in our justice system. They did not do anything other than file the report. Todd was seventeen and it happened in Arkansas, so they said there was nothing I could do. My sister-in-law *hated* me and started calling my home and office to scream at me. She even threatened me and my daughter, stating that she wanted to "slit my throat." It was sickening that no one said anything to her or tried to stop her. They just acted like nothing was wrong.

I took my Jellybean to see a therapist and hoped that she would be able to help heal her broken parts. I knew what my daughter went through but I had never talked to anyone about my own abuse, so I did not know how to help her. Besides, she was so much braver than I had been. I wanted her to get professional help, not my advice, since I failed miserably in helping myself by never speaking about my own abuse. She was the sweetest little girl and seemed like she was doing well in therapy. I fought daily with my husband about my decision to report his nephew and to get our daughter help.

My husband was talked into doing a psych tech program and gone during the day, which was helpful. But when he was home, we fought. He came home less and less. But when he *was* home, it was miserable. I knew he was cheating again and I did not care. I definitely did not want to have sex with him, so his having sex elsewhere took the pressure off me. He had his own paychecks and I paid all our bills.

I was at work one day and one of my coworkers was off and saw him at her apartment complex pool with one of her neighbors. They were playing in the pool and he was kissing her; they appeared to be a happy couple. My coworker asked if I wanted her address so I could go there and catch him in the act. I declined her offer and tried to hide that I was upset and embarrassed. I asked my boss if I could have the rest of the day off and I went home.

I knew he was cheating but having confirmation was strange. I did not know how to feel. Should I congratulate him and his girlfriend, should I wish them well? Would he move in with her, solving all my stress? I wasn't mad—what I felt was more like relief.

When he came home that night I asked, "how was work?" He went on and on about how stressful his day was and how tired he was. I said, "yeah, I know how exhausting swimming can be." He stopped in his tracks and asked "what the hell" I was talking about. I told him that my friend called me; she lives in the same apartment as his girlfriend and now I know. He denied it, of course, and said my coworker was lying. It wasn't worth the fight, so I let it go. But I *knew* and he knew I knew. That was enough. I knew it was just a matter of time till he left and I was OK with that.

21

The Return

Savannah's dad, Harold, made a return to her life, to all of our lives a few years prior. He was an amazing dad to her and not only cared for her but cared for all my children. He would bring them all gifts when visiting our daughter. I loved watching him with my kids. He was the boy I fell in love with all those years ago. I had to keep some distance because my heart still loved him with everything in me. I was miserable in my marriage but I could not allow myself to do what I wanted, which was tell him how I felt, tell him I still loved him. I was married and I had to be free from that first.

His family was wonderful and they all became a part of our life. His mom called me her daughter, and even though Harold and I were not together, she still genuinely loved me. She even loves my children, calling them her grandchildren. This must be where Harold learned to love. His sister Kym called me sister and still does to this day. She is still a dear friend and we have been through so much together. They are a template for how blended families should be, just like my dad and Sharon. There doesn't have to be nastiness and hatred, blended families can be beautiful. Kids see everything we do and it becomes part of who they are as adults and parents. I feel like our behavior is a blueprint for what they will follow later on in life.

The only problem with the blending of my family was my husband. He hated Harold. He talked poorly about Harold, calling him a criminal, a loser who had been in prison. We had many fights about his talking shit about Harold in front of Savannah. It was so wrong. It hurt me as much as it did Savannah. Probably because I was still secretly in love with Harold. In my heart, I knew Harold was a much better man and father than Kenny ever could be.

One day, Harold was dropping Savannah off after a weekend together. She hugged him and ran in the house. I had a bruise around my neck from a fight the night before, about Harold, which turned into me getting hit, choked, and raped again by Kenny, my husband. In his mind, he thought he was proving that he loved me more than Harold ever could, or so he said. He was so twisted and so jealous of Harold.

I had a hooded sweatshirt on but it wasn't high enough to hide the bruises on my neck. Harold noticed the bruising and reached out with concern in his voice, asking, "what the hell?" When he reached towards me I flinched. Not because I was scared of him but because I was conditioned to protect myself. Harold stopped and he had tears in his eyes. He said in a whispered voice that he was sorry and asked, "what did he do to you?" I could not speak. He asked me if my husband was abusing the kids. I told him that I was protecting them (or so I thought). He reached out again, slowly, this time, and took my hand, pulling me close. He wrapped both of his arms around me and held me. I was trying to hold back tears, but something about being in this man's arms made me feel safe. He just held me and cried with me. He whispered, "I love you, Stephanie. Baby, you don't have to put up with this." The only response I could muster was something I held back since I was in the visiting room at the jail, telling him I was pregnant. I said, "I love you, too, Harold, I always have!" His arms closed in tighter around me and I felt safe. I could feel his heart beating, hear his sadness, and I felt his love.

I'm not sure how long we were standing there but Buster came running up from playing with a neighbor and screamed, *"Harold,"* and the moment was over. Harold picked him up and hugged him. Buster, noticing his tears, asked Harold, "Are you crying?" Harold responded, "Yeah, buddy, a little. It's OK for big boys to cry sometimes. I'm just sad that I have to leave and hadn't seen you yet." Buster called him a "dork" and the tickling began.

Joan and Savannah came out and Harold hugged them. They immediately began making plans for his next trip over. There was giggling and laughter. My heart was still beating so fast from hearing him say he loved me and calling me *baby*. I still loved this man with my whole heart.

The hugs were all given and goodbyes all said. He reached out and hugged me and whispered again, "get out of this, baby. If you need help, you know where I am. I love you." I responded with, "I am trying. I love you, too." I think he would have kissed me if the kids were not standing there. I wanted him to. Savannah was smiling, I think she was on to us.

Many years later, she told me that she knew *everything*. He had told her everything about us. It made me happy to know that our daughter knew that her parents always truly loved each other.

22

Kallie and Peggy

My Jellybean, Joan, was in the fourth grade and met some wonderful friends at school and seemed to be thriving. Her best friend was Kallie and one Friday they decided they wanted to spend the night together. Of course, her mom, Peggy, wanted to meet me and I definitely wanted to meet her. So Kallie and Peggy came over and we all met and I adored them both. Peggy was the sweetest and my Jellybean seemed to be really comfortable with her, so I agreed that she could go spend the night at Kallie's. From then on, they were inseparable. It also seemed to help Joan focus on being nine. In those moments, she wasn't thinking about abuse, family drama, or her father's drug habit.

I had told Peggy what had happened to Joan, just so she could look out for her when Joan was with her. I don't know why I was so comfortable with her, but something told me I could trust Peggy. She listened and hugged me and cried with me and said that Joan would be safe and nothing would ever happen to my daughter in her care. It was so comforting to know that someone else besides me was looking out for my child. I don't know if Peggy fully understood how much her love and understanding helped me keep my sanity at that point.

Joan seemed to be thriving and laughing and it did my momma heart good to hear her laugh. It was my birthday and Peggy and her family invited us out to dinner. We all met at a local pizza place in Shell Beach. Of course, my husband was out doing God knows what or who, but I did not care. We all met and had a wonderful dinner and laughed and talked and it was like we were always friends. I loved seeing Joan so happy and smiling, and I was enjoying getting to know my new friend. After a while, it felt like we were sisters, not just friends. I have several sisters, but Peggy was there and listened and cared. Peggy and Kallie and their whole family were a gift from God. Peggy and her husband, Craig, helped so much with my kids. If I needed to get two of them to separate locations, Peggy was there. Kallie and Joan were always together anyway, but knowing she was safe was helpful and gave me so much peace of mind. If Joan wasn't at Kallie's, then Kallie was with us, I'd gained a bonus daughter with the friendship.

Kallie had a brain aneurysm when the girls were in the sixth grade. When Joan called me, sobbing, and said she thought Kallie was going to die, I could barely understand her. I got that they were at the hospital, because Kallie had a seizure, so I went directly to the hospital. I walked into the pediatric ward in time to see Peggy passing out, with Craig catching her. They were talking to a man that appeared to be a doctor. My heart sank—what had she just been told? Was Joan right? Was Kallie dying? God, please, no!

I scanned the room and saw five empty beds and one with Kallie in it. I went straight to Kallie's and sat on her bed. She appeared to be sleeping. I took her hand and thanked God that it was warm. She opened her eyes and smiled. I almost cried. I said, "hey, sweet girl" She smiled with her sweet little smile that could light up the world and said, "I can't remember your name, I know I know you and I know I love you but I can't remember your name." I smiled back at her and said, "well, you remember the important stuff, so you're gonna be just fine." She smiled again and said, "please tell me your name." I tried to hold back the tears but as they started spilling out of my eyes, I said, "It's Steph, your favorite other mother." She smiled and said, "Yes, Stephanie, don't cry!"

Peggy and Craig had finished their conversation with the doctor and returned to Kallie's bed. They looked scared and had red eyes. I hugged them both and both of them were struggling to not sob. I felt blessed to be there and to be told to "please stay" when they told their baby girl that she had to be flown to UCLA to have brain surgery. They were terrified but never showed it. They explained to her that she had a brain aneurysm and explained what it meant in a way that her twelve-year-old mind could understand but not be terrified. And the thing I admired about them was that they *never* wavered in their conviction that she would be OK. They may have been scared or had doubts, but they never showed it. The love they had for each other and their daughter touched my heart and made me fall in love with this family, making us family.

I went home to get Joan so she could see Kallie before she was flown to UCLA. I tried to follow the example Craig and Peggy had set, I kept telling Joan that Kallie would be fine. I don't think Joan could have taken losing her best friend. When we got to Kallie's room, Kallie scooted over in her bed and patted the bed and told

Joan, "You can sleep right here." It made Peggy and I cry. It was comforting to know that Kallie knew who Joan was and that little bit of memory that they slept next to each other was a comforting sign for us.

As we were waiting for the helicopter to come and transport Kallie, the doctor kept asking her questions to determine if she was getting worse or staying the same. He asked her, "what's your mom's name?" She replied, "Mom." He asked, "what's your dad's name?" She replied, "Dad." He asked, "what's your brother's name?" She said, "ummmmmm, Buster." We all laughed and the doctor looked confused, and Peggy told him…close enough.

The helicopter got there and took Kallie for the trip to UCLA and we cried and hugged and Peggy and Craig asked if they could take Joan with them to UCLA. I could not say no. So Peggy, Craig, and Joan went and spent the next three weeks at UCLA. It was so scary, but Kallie was a champ. She survived and I think that experience bonded our families forever.

When Kallie got home she was relieved to be alive but very upset because they had shaved the back of her head. She was twelve, and for a girl to have the back of her head shaved was devastating. We went to Kallie's and my girls both shaved the back of their heads so Kallie wouldn't be so sad. Peggy and Kallie kept saying "no, don't do it." But my girls were set in their conviction to do this. They said, "it's just hair and it will grow back." Kallie cried and then laughed and it did our hearts good to see her smiling. My momma heart was proud.

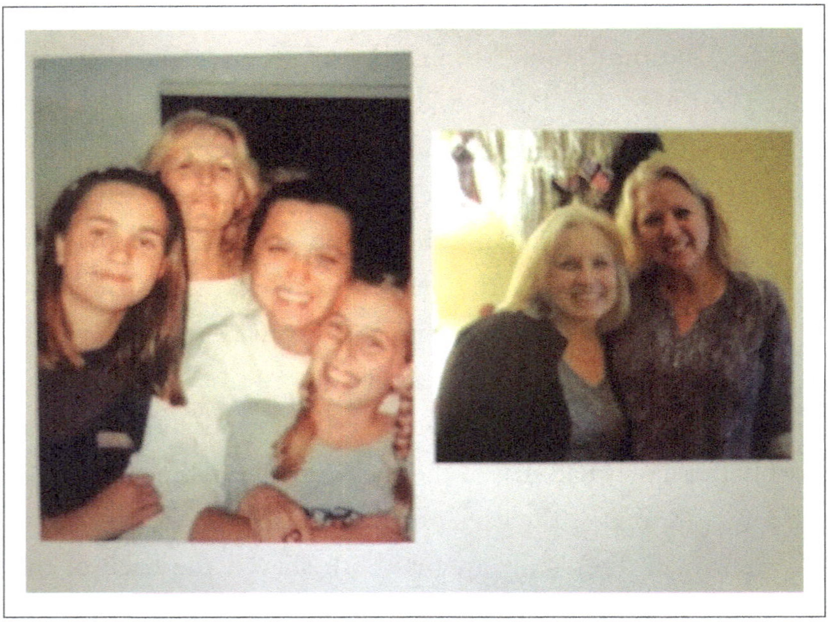

23

Independence Day

One night, shortly after my birthday dinner with Peggy's family, I was in bed sleeping and I heard my husband getting up to use the bathroom. He was in the bathroom when the phone on his nightstand rang. I leaned over and picked it up and it was a woman's voice asking for Kenny. I said, "hold on a sec." Well, now, I thought, this was going to be interesting. I suspected he was using drugs but now also knew he was cheating. He would deny it, of course, when we would fight, and he would adamantly deny it to the point that you would almost believe him, *almost*. I had to keep reminding myself about the STD he gave me, then lied telling me he never had it, that it was me, but I had never slept with anyone but him. Then there was the pool incident that my friend witnessed with her own eyes, that he totally denied. That man lied so much, you could tell he was lying just by the fact he was speaking.

He came into the bedroom and I had the light on his nightstand on and he looked confused. I said, "Your girlfriend is on the phone." He said, "Not this shit again, you psychotic bitch!" I picked up the phone and handed it to him. He put it to his ear and said only *four* words, "hello... yes... no... OK." Then he hung up and, without saying a word, got dressed and left.

After not hearing from him for two days, he called and asked if I was still going to the wedding. That weekend, a friend of his who I did not know was getting married and we had been planning to go. Without hesitation, I told him to fuck off and that he should probably take his girlfriend, and then I hung up. The very next day, I packed up all his clothes and put them out front. I taped a note to them that said, *"these are all yours. If I find more of your things, I will drop them off at your mom's."*

I had the locks changed and waited. The next day was July 4th and I was sitting in the living room having a cup of coffee when I saw him pull up. This is it, here he is, is he gonna blow up, kick the door in, and kill me? I grabbed the cordless phone and was ready to dial 911. My heart was pounding as I silently prayed, "God, please protect my babies; make him leave!" He read the note and loaded the boxes up and left. Thank God. He was gone. The nightmare was over, or so I thought!

It was July 4th, Independence Day, kind of fitting. My friend Keri from work came over and we walked down to Dinosaur Caves Park just down the street. It's a cliff overlooking the Pismo Pier where they were setting off the fireworks. I was free of him. My children were free of their abusive parent and I could not be happier. It was truly *our* Independence Day!

24

Our New Life

We started our new life without my husband and I filed for divorce. His parents were mad at me but they did not have to live with him. I know they wanted me to take him back and live happily ever after, but we were happy without his constant chaos. The kids were coming out of their shells, the shells children live in when one of their parents is unstable, yells, and abuses. They were thriving at school and laughing at home and we were happy on our own.

My mother-in-law was a sweet woman but felt like I needed to "get over our little spat and get back together for the kids' sake." She was blind to the disgusting shit her son did, and blind to the disgusting shit her grandson did to my daughter. She had a heart of gold but would rather not face the truths of the family's dirty little secrets (at least not yet).

The kids were doing great and I loved seeing them emerge into the people they were becoming. Savannah was a bit wild and, at the time, I did not understand her rebellion. I tried to be as understanding as I could but she was grounded a lot. She was an awesome, sweet, wonderful daughter but still a tiny bit wild. I tried to think about what would have got to me at her age and I tried being both her friend and her mother.

Joan was the most obedient, sweet, kind-hearted child and never gave me any arguments. She got great grades and was in school leadership. She and Kallie were into cheerleading and being giddy girls. I enjoyed going to the school to watch them cheer. She seemed happy and asked if she could stop seeing her therapist. I allowed it because I wanted to give her what she wanted. I was in awe of her strength and courage and had a lot of admiration for my sweet baby girl. She was brave, she had stood up to her abuser and I wished I had had her strength when I was little and was abused.

Buster was in youth football and that was awesome for him. Being in a house filled with girls, he needed the boy time and he was rather good at it. I became involved and was on the board and ended up staying involved with youth football for twenty-five years. I only had one son but I always had a bunch of "my boys" over. I still can't go anywhere in town without seeing one of "my boys" or hearing "Momma Steph," and I *love* it.

That first Christmas Eve after Kenny left, the loser showed up on my front door. He was drunk and said he was going to kill himself if he could not be with his kids for Christmas. He looked terrible. He looked like he hadn't eaten in days, had only done drugs, and not slept. Having him sitting in the living room was awkward and even the kids did not really want him there. He started crying and told them he missed our family and he could not wait to be back home with us. He tried to tell the kids that he hoped they liked all the gifts "*we*" had gotten for them. *We?* I was annoyed. I had worked my ass off getting their gifts and I did it alone with no help from him.

I'd finally had enough and told the kids to go to bed. It was late. I went to my daughters' room and told them to keep the door locked and not to unlock it for any reason. Then I went to my medicine cabinet and removed all the medications and brought them to my room. Then I made Buster come into my room to sleep. I went back out to the living room and said that I needed to get to bed, as we were heading to my dad's in the morning and I needed my rest.

He sat there crying and saying how sorry he was for everything, that he wanted to come home and be a family again. I told him that was not possible, that all the abuse, lies, and lack of support from him killed anything we ever had. His begging was ridiculous!! "Please, babe, I love you." I shook my head and said, "no, you could not have ever loved me and done the things you had done to me." If that was his meaning of love, then I did not want any part of it! It had been almost six months since he left and those were wonderful months of growth for me and the kids.

He continued begging, asking that he be allowed to stay the night and be with his children on Christmas morning. I knew there was no way I was going to get him out of my house, so I agreed to let him sleep on the couch but that we were leaving for my dad's at 10:00 a.m. I almost laughed when he said, "I could go with you." I immediately said no, that my dad was not very happy with him and it would be a bad idea. I went and grabbed a spare pillow and blanket, and he was acting distraught when I returned with them. I said, "good night" and as I was walking down the hallway, he said, "I love you." I kept walking, not acknowledging his empty, meaningless claim. I got to my room, locked the door, and was relieved I made it without him trying to hurt me.

Buster was already asleep and I was terrified. I laid there and I could hear him rummaging through the bathroom medicine cabinet and under the sink. He then started the search for money and valuables. My purse was safely in my room and the girls were locked in their room. There were no other valuables because he had stolen and hocked anything of value when we were together. I heard the doorknob being turned and shaken, he was trying to get into my room. I was relieved I had locked the door. It was a very long night. It finally got quiet around two in the morning, and I knew he was asleep or passed out. I had to pee but did not want to open my door, so I quietly cracked the back bedroom door that led outside and I peed out there. I snuggled back in my warm bed with my son sleeping soundly and I thanked God for giving me the strength to stay strong, enabling me to get away from this man. I prayed that he did not find a way in and kill me.

The next morning, Christmas day and Savannah's birthday, I awoke early and snuck out to the living room to get my "Santa" duties done. Kenny was passed out. I made coffee and asked him if he wanted to wake up to watch the kids open their gifts. He mumbled something I did not understand. The kids woke up and the house was buzzing with the excitement of Christmas and what Santa brought. My almost ex-husband slept through it. He had the opportunity to be there with his children and chose to take drugs and pass out and sleep through Christmas morning. Sad!

I made some breakfast and we all sang Happy Birthday to the "best Christmas present ever," my sweet Savannah. She seemed sad and that made me sad. I wanted to ask her what was wrong but I figured it was *him* being there (little did I know why until much later). Joan asked her dad if he wanted to eat but he mumbled something no one could understand. So, we finished up breakfast and the kids all got ready. Being scared to take a shower with him in the house, I brushed my teeth, got dressed, and decided to take a shower when I arrived safely at my dad's house.

I loaded the van with Christmas stuff and the kids and woke him up and said we had to leave. He rolled over on the couch and said, "I will leave after I wake up." I said, no, he had to leave *now*. I told him that my lease clearly states that I could not have people there when I wasn't. It was a lie but I was not about to leave this asshole in my house. He would have taken TVs, VCRs, and computers and hocked them for drug money. And he would then claim it wasn't him, that my house was broken into or some stupid shit.

It was a struggle and he kept acting like he was falling back to sleep so I would say his name louder, "Kenny, we have to leave!" He said he needed a shower first and I said, "No, you've had all morning and I **have to leave now**!" He was pissed and I could see the rage in his eyes. Whatever plan he had cooked up in his head to force himself back into our lives was failing miserably. I had a moment of fear but my landlord was suddenly out front.

We lived on the same property and she came back to our house to give us a loaf of cranberry orange bread. I could hear the kids out front talking to her and peeked my head out to say hi and Merry Christmas. I hugged her and thanked her for the gift and grabbed hers out of the van and she thanked me. I said we were leaving for my dad's and if she could keep an eye on the house, I would appreciate it. She responded with "always, dear." I said it loud enough for Kenny to hear so he knew he could not come sneaking around while we were gone. Then Kenny emerged from the house. As we were chatting, I locked the front door and introduced her to him as the kids' dad, *not* my husband, and she shook his hand and said that his kids were a treasure. A little thing that escaped him since the day he was blessed with them and me. The fact that he slept through Christmas morning with his children was a prime example of why he did not get how blessed he was and chose to toss us all away, preferring drugs and other women.

We all hopped in the van and he went to his car looking like the pathetic shell of a man that he was and I did not feel sorry for him. I had given him the opportunity to spend Christmas with his kids and he *slept* through it. We drove down the long driveway to the street and Buster said, "He's not moving back in, is he?" I said "hell, no." Then Savannah's mood changed. She told me, "Merry Christmas, Mom, I love you." I told her, "Happy Birthday, baby, I love you *forever!*" She smiled for the first time that day and we were off to my dad's.

I thanked God for getting us out of the house safely; I thanked God for that experience. I think it was just what my heart needed to stand strong. To *know* that I had made the right decision to stand up to him and file for divorce. My children and I were thriving without him. For just a moment, I was taken back to the abuse, the lies, the hatefulness of that man, and I was proud that we survived. I should have done it years earlier, like the first time he hit me. That is also a decision I will have to live with, a decision I will regret till the day I die. The horrible things he did when I was not looking, would be later revealed to me.

25

Enter #2

Beginning the new school year, Buster enjoyed playing football and was thriving at it. The girls were doing wonderfully and seemed to be happy. Savannah was still in trouble a lot but nothing too serious, just a little wild. Harold and I had many conversations about her and her behavior. He had gotten married and that broke my heart but what did I expect from him? I guess I had hoped that when I was ready, he would be single and ready to marry me.

One day, I got a call from my gynecologist, he said my annual pap test torture came back with bad cells. I had to go in to talk to him. I went in and he said that he suspected I had cervical cancer and I needed to have a biopsy to check for cancer cells. He said the areas would be removed with the biopsies and we would determine the extent of the cancer. Wait, what?

My heart sank; what would I do if I had to prepare for my death? What would happen to my children? My little brother Joseph had died a couple of years earlier and it devastated my dad; I did not think he would be able to handle losing another child.

I made the call to dad to let him know. He was stunned but happy I had gone. I did not have health insurance, so I kept putting off my annual girl exam. But one day, dad asked if I was keeping up with them. Normally, it would be an odd conversation between a daughter and her dad, but we were close and he had been in the delivery room when I had Savannah, so we did not have the "normal" father/daughter relationship. Ours was better. We were close and often had a sixth sense about one another. When something was going on with the other or if one were sad, the other one could sense it. It's hard to explain other than to give an example: if dad called to say, "hey, don't drive on the 101 today," I would go the back way.

Anyway, he said it was important to stay healthy and he would pay for it if I needed help. He said he could not stand the thought of losing another child. So I found the money and went to get my annual torture and here we were. . . cancer. I had asked my doctor if I could get a second opinion and he said, "yes, who do you want to see and I will arrange it today because I want to do your surgery tomorrow." He said it was fast-spreading but very curable if it was caught early. So I scheduled the surgery for the next day.

Luckily, the cancer cells were all removed and the margins were all clean, so no further treatment was needed. I just had to have the annual torture exam more frequently. I had to go every three months for the first year after, then every six months for two more years, then I could go back to annual. So I guess it's safe to say that my dad's sixth sense saved my life, again.

After the surgery, I was feeling my own mortality. What would happen if the cancer came back? What if I die? I think I got scared that if I died, my kids would have to go to my ex-husband, so I thought maybe I better find someone that will love them and fight to keep them away from Kenny. I had a feeling that Harold would take them, but I wasn't sure his wife would want them. Yes, I know that is a terrible reason to look for a partner.

But I did meet a sweet man. He was one of my sons' coaches. He was not my type *at all*, but he was kind. His nephew and Buster were best friends. He felt safe and I was fearful of men. So safe felt good.

He was very interested and we went out on a couple of dates. He was instantly in love and I cared for him. He was funny and made the kids laugh. So, after a few months of dating, he asked me to marry him and I said yes. I loved him for the kind, giving man he was. I was not "in love" with him; I was comfortable with him. I knew he would never hit me or abuse me mentally, sexually, or physically. He was kind but, still, I knew it was not like the love I had for Harold. So it was not fair to him to have married him. I know that now; I wish I would have known then what I know now. I never set out to hurt this man. It was a loveless marriage for me but he was in love and I will forever regret hurting him.

There was also the "baby" issue. I made it perfectly clear to him that I could not have any babies. I did not want any more babies. Mine were seventeen, fifteen, and twelve. I was *done*. But he still wanted to get married. Then, after the wedding, he started with, "Let's have a baby; we can have your tubes untied." At first, I entertained the idea. I had originally had my tubes tied at twenty-two, when I had my son, because I did not want any more kids. But was it because I did not want any more or because I did not want any more with the asshole I was married to?

Savannah graduated high school, thank God. She was my rebel. She was the one that got arrested, got suspended, snuck out of the house, smoked, drank, tried drugs, and was just a handful all through high school. But, hey, she made it through high school without getting pregnant. She was eighteen, graduated, living on her own, and right next door to me. I found it funny that she spent the last four years trying to get away from me and now we were neighbors. But I liked having her so close and I really liked being able to keep an eye on my baby girl. I loved my first baby girl and we were always close and she has always been one of my best friends.

26

Greatest Blessings

One day, Savannah came over and, in the most serious-sounding tone said, "mom, I need to talk to you." This is it, my daughter is gonna tell me that I am gonna be a grandma, but hey she was eighteen, she graduated, and she would be a great mother. I was thirty-five years old but I was only seventeen when I had her. She took me to my bedroom and we sat on my bed. I *knew* what was coming, I just wanted her to come out and say it. She took my hands and looked right at me. Here was my precious first-born child struggling to tell me that she was pregnant. I think I was smiling as I was remembering telling my parents that I was pregnant and how terrified I was.

I finally said, "What?" then she dropped a bomb… "Mom, Joan is pregnant!" I did not understand who she was talking about, so I asked, "Joan who?" Savannah said, "Joan, your daughter." Wait, what? My sweet little sixteen-year-old baby girl who never even talked back, Joan?" I'm sure I looked shocked and there was an awkward moment of silence as I tried to switch gears and process that Savannah was not the one that was pregnant, but Joan was. Then, Joan walked into the room and was crying. She said, "I'm sorry, Mom." She sat down next to me and I hugged my sweet little four-pound baby girl and I told her exactly what my parents told me: "Joan, don't cry; it's a baby and a baby is a blessing. I love you no matter what." It's weird how I was having the same conversation with my parents in a similar situation at the same age. I just wanted her to know she was loved and there was no judgement, no disappointment, just a momma's love, *forever*!

So, after the tears and hugs, I asked how far along she was, thinking she was gonna say six to eight weeks and she said, "six months, I think." I was worried. She had not yet been to the obstetrician. So I told her we needed to get her in to see the doctor tomorrow to make sure the baby was growing OK. She was relieved; I was in shock. Six months pregnant. So, I'm gonna be a grandma in three months! I was never fearful. I knew Joan could do it! She was way stronger and way braver than I ever could be and she had *me*! I was gonna make sure that she was ok and my grandbaby was gonna be *exactly* what I told her, *a blessing*."

We went to see her OB-GYN and they did an ultrasound and we got to see the baby and hear the heartbeat. He was perfect! My grandson, EJ. So blessed!!

He was as excited to see us as we were to see him, and he came five weeks early, just like his uncle Buster. Joan had a difficult labor and after about twenty-four hours in labor, they decided to take him via C-section. He was so precious and I could not believe that I was a grandma. They ended up calling me Nana and that was great with me. It's what EJ could say when he got old enough to speak and it stuck, I liked it.

When Joan was in the hospital, after having EJ, Savannah stayed the night with her, which I found precious. I loved that my daughters had always been close. I went to the hospital and brought the girls breakfast. When I got to the hospital, Savannah was in a foul mood and said that she had been up all night, sick as hell. Turns out Savannah was pregnant with my second grandchild, she just did not know it yet. About two weeks later, Savannah got confirmation that she was pregnant. I was thrilled. Another baby, another blessing.

When EJ was eight months old, Savannah called me and said she thought she had the flu, that she had been up all night feeling sick and had stomach cramps. I said, "Why don't we get you to the hospital and see if the baby is OK." I figured she was in labor but, if not, she probably needed to be hydrated after being sick all night. Her boyfriend had already left for work, so I volunteered.

I went to get her and we drove down to Santa Maria to where she was registered. They took her directly up to Labor and Delivery, hooked up an IV, did a cervical check, and said, "well, Savannah, you're having a baby *today*." She was already dilated to six centimeters. She called her boyfriend, Ryan, and said, "Get here, quick." They were prepping her, hooking her up to monitors, and calling her doctor.

I was excited and called my husband, kids, and Savannah's dad. Everyone was waiting patiently. Savannah is a rock star! Door-to-delivery in one hour! She was starting to push when Ryan got there. He had one leg, I had the other, and the doctor said, "OK, now that we are all here, the party of four is about to get a fifth. Push, Savannah!" A few pushes and Hailey entered the world. I could not speak; there were no words. I had never been in a delivery to witness a baby being born. I had when my children were born, obviously, but it's a whole different experience to witness.

Hailey was perfect and beautiful. She looked exactly like her momma did when she was born. It took me a few minutes to be able to speak. I was overwhelmed with emotions and happiness. I have a granddaughter. My perfectly matched set, EJ and Hailey. They joked later that they were the *Original Grandbabies*, the OGs, as EJ claimed. They were the most precious gifts I could ever have, next to their mommas. I felt so much happiness and felt truly blessed.

27

Goodbye, Mother

So my sister, Jen, had stayed close with both my mom and older brother. I kept my distance to keep my sanity and to keep protecting my heart from being ripped out or broken by her. Jen called to let me know our mother had a stroke. She was not doing well and was in the hospital.

Mother had been in a car accident when she was young and she almost died. She had a metal plate in her head from the surgery performed the night of the accident. She was never the same after. I often wondered if her mental issues were from that trauma or if she was just a mean, hateful person. I knew she was bipolar years before she was actually diagnosed.

I remember the phone call back then from my sister, Jeffi. She was in tears and said that mom was diagnosed with bipolar disorder, and seemed shocked and devastated. I reminded her that I had told her mom was bipolar ten years ago and asked why she was crying about it. It wasn't like her mother was just diagnosed with a terminal disease, she would be fine. Jeffi was upset with me and felt like I was callous about it. I explained to my sister that I earned my callouses and asked if she remembered what her mother did to me. Jeffi did but she did not want to talk about it. Ignoring Mother's behavior was what everyone did.

When Jeffi called with the news that Mother was in the hospital, I knew that I had to go and make peace with her. Not for her sake, but for my own heart and my own peace of mind. I had learned a lot about bipolar disorder and knew that between that and her brain injury, she was not in control, especially of her emotions when I was a child as she tortured me daily.

Bipolar disorder is a mental disorder caused by structural and functional changes in the brain or changes in genes. Affected individuals like my mother experience episodes of depression and episodes of mania. Bipolar disorder lasts for a lifetime, with treatments aiming at managing the symptoms by psychotherapy and medication. Bipolar disorder was once known as manic depression.

The manic phase is characterized by:

- Extreme happiness, hopefulness, and excitement
- Irritability, anger, *fits of rage, and hostile behavior (don't I know this part of the disease)*
- Restlessness
- Agitation
- Rapid speech
- Poor concentration and judgment
- Increased energy
- Less need for sleep
- Unusually high sex drive

- Setting unrealistic goals
- Paranoia

The depressive phase may include:

- Sadness and crying
- Feelings of hopelessness, worthlessness, and guilt
- Loss of energy
- Loss of interest or pleasure in everyday activities
- Trouble concentrating and making decisions
- Irritability (this was constantly directed at me)
- Need for more sleep or sleeplessness
- Change in appetite; weight loss/gain
- Suicidal thoughts and attempts at suicide

Patients may feel normal, without any symptoms, in between episodes of mania and depression.

As much as I wanted to hate my mother forever, I knew in my heart that she was sick. I could not justify being mad at an epileptic for having a seizure, so I had to forgive mother for the actions that I endured because of her bipolar disorder.

I went to the hospital where she was at and walked into her room. She was not the monster I remembered. She was weak and frail and seemed small. When she was torturing me, she seemed larger than life, she seemed evil and Satanic. I walked into her room and just stood there for a few minutes, silently, and observed her. She opened her eyes and looked right at me and she looked sad. This articulate woman, that was so intelligent, so educated, who had a Master's degree in education (which I found hilarious, why would a woman who hated her own daughter want to be a teacher?).

But here she was and now she could not even form a sentence. The stroke had affected her speech and right side. Her hand was curled up and her face was droopy.

She held her hand up and tried to speak but she was struggling, so I walked closer and said, "hi, Mom." She stopped struggling and motioned that she wanted me to sit in the chair by her bed. So I sat down and said that Jeffi had called me and told me she was here. It was terrible to see her struggle to speak. I looked into her eyes and saw so much sadness, I think it was regret she was feeling. She was medicated now for her bipolar disorder and she *was* smart, so I am sure she was struggling with the shit she did to me. At least to me, it seemed like she was feeling regret.

I saw tears in her eyes and saw her struggling to speak. I reached out and took her hand and said, *"Mom, it's OK. I know you were sick and I know that you did the best you could with what you had and I am OK. I have a wonderful life and amazing children and two grandchildren. I turned out OK, I'm fine and I forgive you."* She began to cry and even though she could not speak words, her tears spoke volumes. Somehow, in that moment, we communicated like we never had before. I held her hand, the hand that had inflicted so much pain on me, and it looked different. It looked weak and not so terrifying.

I asked her if she would like for me to come back and visit the next weekend and she nodded and seemed to really want that. I went back the next weekend and Savannah went with me along with my sweet grandbaby, Hailey. My grandmother came as well and we took a five-generation picture. Mother died shortly after that.

I was really happy that I was able to let go of the anger I had for her. I did not want to carry that anger for the rest of my life and if I had not forgiven her when she was alive, then I would have carried it forever. I did not want the abuse she inflicted upon me to define who I was. I was happy that I was able to let her know that I forgave her. I had to, for my own heart and my own peace of mind. When she died, at least she knew she was forgiven by me. She still had to answer to God, but I feel He is much more forgiving than I am. After all, I'm far from perfect and he loved my mother for the perfect child of God that she once was, that he created her to be.

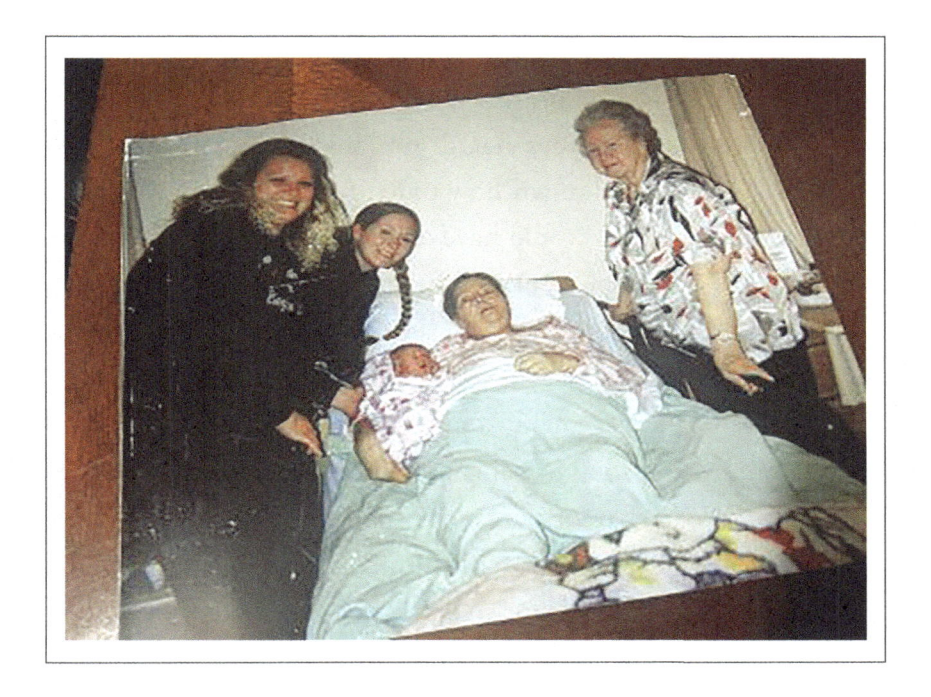

28

EJ and Hailey—OGs

I had always heard grandparents say, "if I would have known how much fun being a grandparent was, I would have done it first." Which I thought was ridiculous, but after becoming a Nana, I understood. Grandchildren truly are the most amazing blessings any woman can receive.

EJ was growing and such a sweet baby. Buster loved him and took to being an uncle. One night, I heard EJ fussing. I went out to the living room and Buster was walking the floor with him. I asked, "what's up?" and Buster said, "Joan is exhausted, so I wanted to let her sleep." He melted my heart with his love and kindness to his sister, the same sister he tortured for years when they were growing up.

The kids may have fought when they were young, but they did love each other. We were all we had, so we had to stick together. I felt blessed that they were going to have each other when raising their own children. EJ and Hailey were funny together, more like brother and sister. I remember them coming together to the football field and running around. Hailey was eight months younger but she was fast and could outrun EJ, and that irritated him. He thought that since he was older, he should always be bigger and faster.

I loved to have them both over and do the Nana thing, which was to spoil them and send them home so I could rest. I was still young. I was thirty-eight, but my babies had their own babies. I was grateful that I was young enough to keep up with them because they were a handful. People used to mistake me for their mom. I loved to say, "no, I'm his Nana," or "I'm her Nana."

As I watched my daughters become mothers, I felt so much pride. They were amazing mothers and as hard as I felt we had it, I believed I must have done something right for them to turn out to be so good at being mammas. Even my son, he wasn't a parent yet, but I knew down deep he would be great at it. I remember thinking that I had failed as a mother because my children had only the bare necessities growing up. I struggled to keep a roof over their heads and food on the table. They did not have the latest, greatest shoes or clothes. I was barely able to make ends meet but they never went without. But I did feel bad that I had failed to give them an amazing childhood. Then, one day, I was listening to Buster talk to a friend about how wonderful his childhood was, and I asked him, "You think your childhood was good?" He said, "hell yah, Momma, we had a blast." So I felt a bit of happiness that he hadn't noticed the lack of monetary things, he was just happy. I guess that makes me very successful.

29

Justice, Finally— Kinda

We still got to see my niece LeeAnne. She is the niece I was closest to. She went back and forth to and from Arkansas with us. She lived with us for a long time because her mom was nuts and put her head through a wall when she was in Junior High. LeeAnne was an awesome kid and grew up to be an awesome mom. She was married now and just had twins. Kinda funny because she was a handful as a child and I remember telling her that if God was just, when she was pregnant, He would make them twins, and, viola, twins it was. She was a great mom and had her hands full. Her husband already had four children from a previous marriage but LeeAnne took the awesome mom route and blended her family and loved her stepchildren. LeeAnne's brother was Todd, the asshole who molested my Joan.

LeeAnne came to us one day and said that she wanted to apologize because when I filed charges against her loser brother and it caused such a rift in the family, she did not want to believe that about her brother. That is, until her brother molested her oldest stepdaughter. She was pissed and heartbroken and I'm sure she was embarrassed as well.

So we were finally able to go to court. They were not adding to his charges but the District Attorney in Tulare County had more balls than the DA in San Luis Obispo County, and they wanted to make the court aware of Todd's past. They called and asked Joan to write a statement to read about what he had done to her as a child and how it impacted her life.

We talked about it. I wasn't sure if she would want to be in the same room with him. But, like the incredibly strong amazing warrior she is, she said yes, absolutely she wanted to. She was not sure she wanted to read it but she wanted to be there while the judge read it. She worked on her victim impact statement for several days. I took the day off and we traveled all the way to Visalia for court.

We went into the courtroom with my niece and her husband and—no surprise—Joan's grandparents (Kenny's parents) were there in support of the child-molesting grandson and my former sister-in-law (LeeAnne and Todd's mom). It was awkward because the grandparents hugged me, Joan, and my niece, like we were just there to have lunch together and catch up. Talk about an elephant in the room that no one wanted to recognize. I wanted to say, will you guys admit *now* that that little pervert is a child molester?! But I did not! They *never* wanted to discuss reality and face it; it was easier for them to ignore the shitty stuff.

It came time for the pervert to make his statement and he went on and on about how the victim was a willing participant and they loved each other, and how he would never touch a child or anyone that did not want him to. I sat there, thinking that the only truthful thing that came out of his mouth was his name. I kept my arm around Joan just so she would know she was not alone, that her mother loved her and believed her and would *never* let anyone hurt her again.

Then the DA had his turn. He said that the defendant had, in fact, done this previously and that the victim was sitting in the courtroom and had written a statement that he wanted the judge to read. Todd dropped his head and stared at the floor. The judge asked to see Joan's letter and took a few minutes to read it. Joan was quietly crying, but I was so proud of her for her bravery, for overcoming what that pathetic little pervert did to her. I kept looking over at the pervert and wanted to shout out, *not such a big man now, are you asshole?* You're a big punk picking on a baby girl when you're all alone in the dark of night. "Never done this before," my ass. How many little girls have you messed with, you disgusting pervert. *You lose*, she survived you! Of course, I did not, but I had dreams about doing it for a long time.

The judge finished reading and thanked Joan for her statement and her bravery, and Todd was sentenced. Not for long enough, but the little pervert was going to jail and he was going because my daughter was a badass brave warrior. If I had not filed charges back when I first found out, then her statement never would have been admitted and he would have been a "first time offender." So, I was so relieved that I had made that decision. I had to stand *alone*, against this *entire* family when I filed the charges and a lot of them hated me for it. Most just ignored his sick behavior. But if I had to do it over again, I wouldn't have it any other way. I was standing up for *my* daughter because she needed someone to have her back and

I had promised her in that NICU to *always* protect her. Although I failed because this pervert hurt her, I was never going to let her fight alone.

We left the courtroom and my former sister-in-law was *pissed* and walked away from us. My former in-laws gave hugs all around and tried to be polite but my former mother-in-law said, "It did not have to be like this, his life is ruined," as she was holding back tears. And all I could think was, you're right, it did not *have* to be this way, that pervert did not have to touch my baby, this family did not *have* to protect him, and shame on *all* of you because it's all *your* fault that he was able to victimize another girl. Instead, I simply said, "you're right, he did not *have* to molest my daughter. He made that choice and the choices you make dictate the life you lead!"

Joan and I left and met my niece and her husband at a local restaurant. We were going to have some lunch with them before heading back to the coast. Joan seemed relieved; I was a mixed bag of emotions. I wanted to kill the pervert. I wanted to slap his disgusting, disturbed mother. I wanted to shake my former-in-laws and say "wake up folks. Open your eyes to how much you all turn a blind eye to. *Stop enabling this sick shit!*"

As we were getting our food to the table, LeeAnne's phone began buzzing. Her twisted mother was calling and demanding to know where we were because she wanted to come down and tell *me* a few things. Everyone could hear her through the phone because she was screaming. LeeAnne just said "no, Mom." Not sure what that psycho wanted to *tell me*. Her son was a pervert; he molested not only *my* child but another child. She found out about it and blamed me and my child, who was ten at the time. She was always a psycho but, as a mother, how do you not see the sickening pattern? I guess no mother wants to believe her child is capable of evil, but when a pattern is established, why attack the victim or the victim's mother?

My heart broke for my niece because her mother was nuts, but I was so proud of the woman and mom she had become. I wanted to take some credit, because she was with me more than her mother over the last half of her life. LeeAnne came from crazy like I had, and yet, she survived that crazy and did not turn into the psycho her mother was. I loved my niece like she was my oldest child and hated to see the pain she was in. I could not imagine my brother being a pedophile and abusing one of my children.

30

Kenny's Death

Soon after the court case, LeeAnne had come to tell us that my ex-husband, Kenny, was not doing well. He had killed his liver with drugs, alcohol, and hepatitis. LeeAnne wanted us to know so the kids could decide if they wanted to say goodbye. I had learned how important forgiveness was through losing my own mother. I left this decision up to my children. I was not going to his house to offer my forgiveness but I told my children that I would not take it as a show of disrespect to me if they wanted to go see him.

My son was adamant that he was not going. He said, "That man walked away from me, was horrible to us, and is already dead to me!" Joan was a different story, which did not surprise me because she had a gentle heart. She took my grandson and went to see her dad. He got to meet our grandson and chat with our daughter. After he died, Joan put him up on a pedestal. She was struggling with losing her dad. Her dad was never available and when he was present, he was a nightmare. But I was not going to take away her need to grieve in her own way.

It was shocking to see some of her posts, I wondered, who are you talking about? Because my ex-husband was *not* the wonderful father she was making him out to be. Even my dad called and asked who the hell she was talking about. But I continued to let her mourn her father.

We went to the funeral, even Buster went. He decided to make peace and say his goodbyes so we all went. Buster and I talked before we left and he asked if he was wrong for not being sad. I told him he was not wrong, that his dad was not really ever a part of his life and when he *was* there, he was a mean, hateful person, so not crying about it was OK. But at least he was able to come to the funeral and say goodbye. I still have never told him everything his father did to me. They were burdens a young boy should never have to face. So I am sure, when he reads this, he will be sad or mad or both. Had he known, I think Buster would have refused to be at Kenny's funeral. Buster was and still is fiercely protective of me and his sisters.

Joan was devastated and cried. But I did not say anything, and I did not take it as a betrayal, she had no clue either about what her father did to me. The funeral was mostly painless and we came home with that part of our life closed, or so I thought!

When EJ was five, Joan met a man and they decided to get married. I did not like the man, but Joan loved him. She was an adult and there was nothing I could do but wish her the best and let her know I was always there for her. Something really bothered me about this man, and I was fearful for my daughter and grandson. And having them move-out was like having my heart ripped out. I remember telling a coworker that Joan was moving out and she was taking the baby, and my co-worker laughed and said, "he's her son; what did you expect? that she would leave him?" I accepted that they were leaving but planned to visit a lot. They were moving an hour away, so I was lucky that they weren't moving across the country.

Joan got married and seemed happy, she never let on that her husband was an asshole. She was trying to have another baby before she realized what an idiot her husband was. Joan got pregnant twice and lost both babies. It was devastating for her. There are never enough correct words that can be said to comfort that kind of heartache. My heart broke for my daughter; there is nothing harder than watching your child grieve.

I tried to be there for her, but her being an hour away made it difficult. I kept in touch with her by phone and we *loved* the weekends that I got to take my sweet EJ for a few days. He used to get in my car and talk the entire hour it took to get to my house but I *loved* every second. Apparently, he had a lot to fill me in on. I remember how smart he was, He was very mature for a child and he always seemed smarter than average. I also noticed what a tender heart he had. He felt things very deeply, like his momma. I was so blessed to have such an amazing grandson.

31

Greatest Loss

I had been talking with Harold quite a bit over the last several years and he was a great listener. He loved my children like they were *all* his. I told him about my fears with Joan's husband and he understood because of what I had gone through with her dad. He told me things that were meant for just us forever, so I can't share, I must keep them safe in my heart. We were close again like the best friends we used to be. We were both married but neither of us were happy. We had a love that I still can't explain. I just knew that if time and circumstances were different, we would be together and I was patiently waiting for that day and I believe he was as well.

One day I heard that Harold's brother had died. I called him right away and we talked for hours. He had called me when he heard about my brother's death and he told me that he remembers calling me to offer condolences but had no idea the pain I was enduring till now. We talked and cried and laughed at some memories of his brother from when we were kids. It was such a wonderful phone call and it lasted for almost two hours. When we were hanging up, he said that losing his brother Mike made him not *ever* want to take one single day for granted. Then, there was a pause and he said, "I love you, Stephanie; I want you to know that I *really, really* love you and I can't thank you enough for our friendship and our daughter." I said, "I *really, really* love you, too, you dork and thank you for giving me the greatest Christmas gift *ever*!" We hung up and that was our last conversation. Shortly after this call, he was struck and killed while riding his motorcycle.

When Harold died, it was like a part of me died. I felt numb and lost. We had loved each other since I was sixteen. It was a rare and precious love that cannot be matched. His sister, Kym, called to tell me Harold had died and asked if I could tell Savannah because she just could not. I called our daughter and asked her to come over right away. She said she was heading to her dad's, she had heard he was in an accident. I asked her to come to my house first, that it was very important. She was there within five minutes and I walked out front; by the look of my red, swollen eyes, she *knew*! She got out of the car and she just said, "no, Mom, no," as we embraced and I said, "he's gone, baby." We cried together right there in my front yard, trying to console each other. I told her how much he loved her and she told me, "he loved you, too, mom, he always loved you." It was one of the hardest days of my life. I lost the love of my life and my heart ached for him and for our daughter's grief.

It did not seem fair that such a wonderful man had been taken so young. I was angry with God. Why take Harold? Why not a murderer or child molester? Why take such a good man from the people who loved him? Why had I not left Kenny sooner and married this man I loved? He had asked, we discussed starting a new life together. *Why*, God, had I not just been brave and jumped at the chance with him? Would things be different? Would he still be alive? My heart had a thousand questions *why* and no relief from the pain of my soul breaking in two.

32

Baby Nahla

Savannah had gotten married and she was pregnant with grandbaby number three, and we were all thrilled. It felt like a bright spot in a dark few years for our family. Savannah was happy and her baby bump was growing. She called me one day and said that they were taking Nahla via C-section and could I come hold her while she was under anesthesia because she did not want baby Nahla to die alone. I was on the football field and was so confused; the questions were piling up. Wait, what? Why would baby Nahla die? She was early, but modern technology was amazing and being a preemie was not a death sentence. Why were they taking her via C-section?

I told my husband and Buster that I had to leave, that Savannah was having the baby, and ran off the field to go the thirty minutes to San Luis Obispo to straighten this out!! Maybe Savannah misunderstood her doctor.

I arrived at the hospital in time to see and talk with my daughter and the doctor. Apparently, she had been having weird pains for the last month, in addition to having stroke-level blood pressure which caused her liver to shut down, triggering liver failure, and causing a lack of oxygen to baby Nahla, which would lead to her inability to survive outside the womb without medical support. It was also the reason that Savannah had to have a C-section, as her body could not physically endure labor without having a stroke or dying.

Savannah and my son-in-law had made the difficult decision to let Nahla live until she stopped breathing. They did not want to put her on a respirator, as she wouldn't live long, even with that aid. I could not imagine having to make that decision. Savannah asked me to make sure that Nahla was held continuously and not left alone. She would try to wake up and be able to hold her before she died. I promised her that she wouldn't be alone and I would tell her all about her mama. She was wheeled into the OR as I waited, prayed, and cried.

I was lucky that my Joan was there with me. I think we gave each other strength. We were in Savannah's room with Buster and my son in-law and they brought this tiny little one-pound baby in and handed her to her daddy. Everyone got the chance to hold her and kiss her perfect, beautiful face. Everyone said their goodbyes and my son in-law got her back and he was staring at her and Nahla took a deep breath and I think it startled him. He started handing her back to the nurse and I think the nurse saw the look on mine and Joan's faces. We were *not* handing her over to die alone in a crib. The nurse asked if we wanted to hold her in another room and Joan and I said yes.

She led us to another room and Joan and I loved on her, talked to her, told her all about her momma and sister. Joan lovingly and gently changed her diaper and swaddled her up all warm and snuggly and handed her to me. I was in awe of my brave daughter and my heart was breaking for her as well. Here she had lost two babies and never even had this kind of time with them but she was giving her sister's baby all the love she could before saying goodbye. Joan's strength made her a rock and my hero.

I was rocking her and told her that I would take care of her mom and sister if she would take care of her grandpa Harold for me. I was singing her a song that I sang to all my grandbabies when I felt her leave this world. That wonderful nurse came in and, as I was finishing the alphabet song, she confirmed that Nahla was gone. My heart was breaking. This sweet little baby lived for two hours and died in my arms.

I was so grateful that Joan and I had that time with her. I was so glad that I was not alone while saying goodbye to one of my grandchildren. This was not the appropriate order in life, I was supposed to go first.

I held her a little longer and whispered to her how much she was loved, and kissed her and I cried. When the nurse came back in to take her, Joan and I went back across the hall to Savannah's room. Everyone was looking at us and I let them all know that she was gone. There were tears and hugs and everyone began departing. I was waiting for Savannah to get out of the recovery room.

When they wheeled her in, it was just me and her husband. She looked at me and asked, "where is she?" I looked at her and it broke my heart to tell her that Nahla was gone but she was never alone, she was with me and Joan and I was rocking her and singing to her when she went to heaven. The sadness in my daughter's eyes broke my heart. God, how much does this child have to take? How much more before she nutted up? I hugged her and asked if she wanted to see Nahla. She did, and so I told the nurse and she brought my baby, her baby. There are no words to describe that kind of pain and there are definitely not enough words to describe watching my daughter go through that kind of pain, more grief.

Joan was wonderful in helping her sister through this. We had to plan a funeral but my daughter was broken. She was in pain from having a C-section, pain in her heart from losing her daughter, pain from her milk coming in and no baby to feed it to. It was heartbreaking.

Harold's family came to stay for a week, and I appreciated the support. We were family, the way it should be. Through divorces, separations, custody, frustrations, and then there were the kids. We were all there because we all loved a baby who never stepped foot on this earth. And that is how it should *always* be. A blended family.

I went to the funeral home with Joan and Buster. We picked out a casket. It was beautiful, so tiny and pink. I never knew that they had tiny caskets for children.

The thought of her tiny, perfect little body and beautiful face kept flooding my heart and mind. Several times, it became overwhelming and I would feel my son or my daughter's hands on my back. We were all devastated. Joan picked out a beautiful dress for her to be buried in and had the pamphlet prepared for the service. It was beautiful. I got some flowers from one of Nahla's dad's friends who owned a nursery and I prepared the flowers for her casket and service. We had several pink gerber daisies left over, so I saved them to bring to the service for the family. Savannah's Aunt Kym, Harold's sister, went and picked out the plot.

The night before the service, we were all at Savannah's and the Bishop from the church came to discuss the service and requests from Nahla's parents. We had history with the Bishop, as he was also a teacher and served as the principal at the high school, and had Savannah in his office many times. I opened the door and let him into our full house and made some introductions that would have confused most people. We have such a weird blend of family.

Here was Savannah's ex (Hailey's dad). Her husband, her grandparents, her Aunt Kym and her daughters, Hailey's other grandmother, me and Buster and Joan and my husband. After all the introductions, the Bishop said, "OK, ummmm." I said, don't try to figure this all out, we are *family* and it works for us." He chuckled and asked if he could pray with us. His prayer was beautiful and he prayed for our weird family with all its dynamics and asked our Heavenly Father to ease our broken hearts.

The funeral was heartbreaking and I was not sure I could be strong for my family. Again, there is no way to describe the pain of watching your child grieve. The bishop spoke and my Joan was going to share a poem. How on earth was she able to do it? I was again in *awe* of my daughter's strength. After all, she was still in pain following the loss of her own babies, and yet here she stood to read a beautiful poem for her sister's baby.

Footprints
Author Unknown

"These are my footprints,
So perfect and so small.
These tiny footprints
Never touched the ground at all.

Not one tiny footprint,
For now I have wings.
These tiny footprints were meant
for other things.
You will hear my tiny footprints,
In the patter of the rain.
Gentle drops like angel's tears,
Of joy and not from pain.
You will see my tiny footprints,
In each butterflies' lazy dance.
I'll let you know I'm with you,
If you just give me the chance.
You will see my tiny footprints,
In the rustle of the leaves.
I will whisper names into the wind,
And call each one that grieves.
Most of all, these tiny footprints
Are found on Mommy and Daddy's hearts,
'Cause even though I'm gone now,
We'll never truly part."

I felt and heard the pain in Joan's voice as she stood there and read the poem. Her voice cracked once and there was a pause, and her Aunt Kym walked over and put her arm around her and that gave Joan the strength to finish. Kym is technically only Savannah's aunt, but Kym loves all my children like they were her brother Harold's children. And that is what a *family* does.

My parents' words were ringing in my head. "The more people that love your children, the better off your children will be." I felt so blessed that so many people loved my children. They were raised by a single mamma but they had so many other people that loved and treasured them and those people were family.

I remember feeling numb, like I could not take seeing my children grieve anymore. I looked down to my left and saw my son and daughters and husband and they all had tears rolling down their faces. I knew I had to be strong but I felt weak. I felt a hand on my shoulder and turned and saw my friend Brandi, with tears in her eyes. I remember thinking wait, aren't you on vacation? My dear friend came home from vacation to be supportive. How could I not glean strength from the love of my friends and family? I was truly broken but felt so blessed.

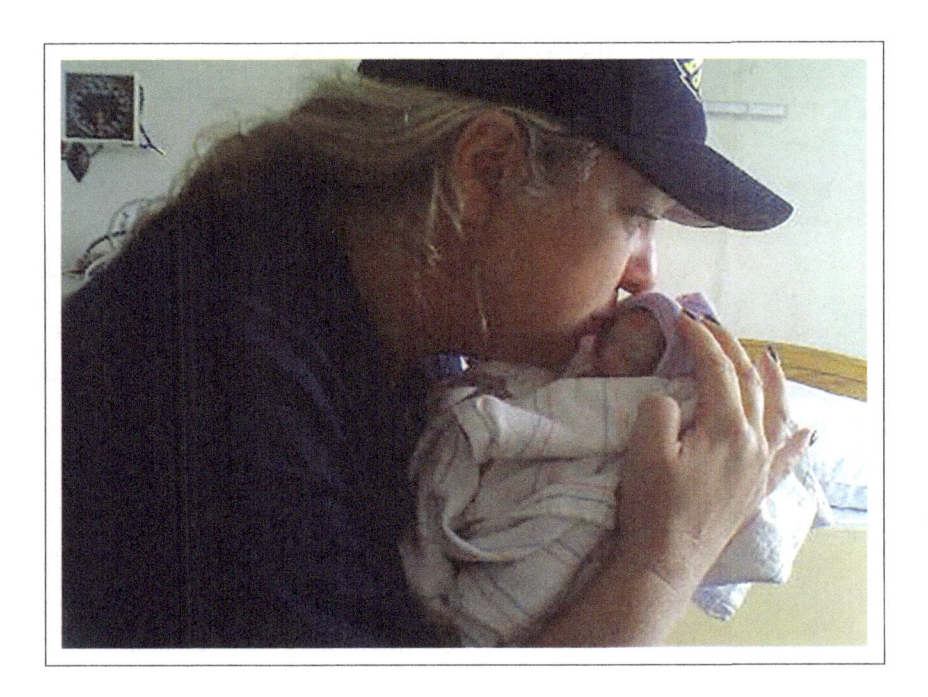

33

Kylie

Savannah was incredibly strong and began living life again. She and I got matching tattoos of Nahla's footprints on our feet, that way, she would always walk with us. My first tattoo in my 40s. All my kids had them, but this was my first, and it had a lot of meaning.

Savannah found out that she was pregnant again and was very fearful, she still had the fresh wounds from losing Nahla. She was considered high risk and was monitored a lot. She called me one day and said, "it doesn't feel like the baby is moving." We immediately went to the doctor. He ordered an ultrasound and we went to go get it and talked about *everything* except what was on both our minds. Was the baby OK?

We went in to the ultrasound facility; they allowed me to go in with her and I was holding her hand. We saw the baby formed and looking perfect, except, wait, where is the heartbeat? No heartbeat, no movement. The tech said, "ok, my dear, we are done here. We will send the doctor your results." Savannah quietly got up and went to get dressed.

I asked the tech, "was the volume down? I did not hear a heartbeat." She said "no, sadly the baby's heart is not beating." She apologized and Savannah came out and was ready to go. She knew, she just did not want to say it out loud. The drive home was quiet until Savannah said, "there was no heartbeat, Mom." Her tears started and so did mine. We cried and talked and I tried my best to comfort her. We got to her house and she called the doctor. We waited for him to call back. He called and confirmed that the baby's heartbeat had stopped and they would need to go in and take out the fetus. They scheduled her an appointment for Monday; it was only Friday. Savannah was pissed and asked, "so I have to carry my dead baby in my body through the weekend?" She was devastated.

She called her husband and told him the news. She opened a bottle of wine and we shared the bottle. She said since it wouldn't hurt the baby, she needed a glass of wine with her momma. We talked and laughed and found comfort knowing Nahla and this baby would be with her dad in heaven.

I could not help but think of Harold holding the babies, all four of them that Joan and Savannah had lost. I laughed, thinking about how he always said he wanted four boys and up there he was with four babies. I knew he was loving them as I would have here on earth, but I did look up and say, "ok, that is enough grandbabies for you; let us keep a few, please." I said a prayer that night to God and asked that that be enough for my daughters to endure. I prayed for strength to help my girls and asked him to kiss our newest angel from her Nana.

Savannah's husband worked out of town during the week so I spent a lot of nights over there with her and we had a lot of talks about life and how precious it was. We talked about family and friends. It was precious healing time. I loved that my daughter wanted me around and I loved that we were best friends and could tell each other everything. I did feel like she was holding something back, but I did not push. I have never lost a child, like she had, so maybe that was what I was sensing. I endured the pain of abuse at the hands of my grandfather, mother, and ex-husband but I did not know the pain my daughters had endured with the loss of their precious babies. Regardless, I was gonna be there when she was ready to talk.

One day, many months later, I was at Savannah's and I thought I saw a baby bump. She noticed me staring. She was pregnant!!! She wanted to wait for the second trimester before getting her hopes up or telling the crazy family we had. The pregnancy went smooth and the doctor was going to attempt to let her deliver naturally. Anyway, that was the plan.

She called me one day and said that her husband was out of town but she thought she might be in labor. I dropped everything and went to get her and took her to the doctor. Sure enough, she was in labor but there was a problem. *Of course there was a problem.* I was suddenly frightened and then the doctor said that all was OK, the baby was fine. Savannah, however, was not. Her blood pressure was way too high, so for Savannah's safety, they had to take the baby via C-section. That is was OK with me—no one dies today!!!!

Her husband was on his way back from Simi-Valley where he worked and I thought, well, if he doesn't make it, I'll get to see the birth of another grandbaby. He made it but I still got to see her right after. Beautiful rainbow baby Kylie Ann was born and we could not be happier. (A rainbow baby is the first pregnancy following a miscarriage.) Momma and baby were healthy and they both survived; that is more than we had over the last several years. I thanked God for this blessing.

Kylie had the face of an angel and I could not help but call her Angel Face. She was a beautiful baby and so sweet. She loved her big sister and grew like a happy healthy baby should.

34

Heart Attack

My second husband and I were still married and he was a great friend. He loved me and I knew he did. I did not ever worry about him being mean, hitting me, or cheating. But I was not in love with him. I loved him but that head-over-heels in love relationship was not there for me. And because it wasn't there for me, I started getting annoyed at things. Things that wouldn't otherwise bother me if we had just remained friends.

He was wonderful, but immature. I used to tell him to "stop acting twelve," "put your hat on straight," "you're not thirteen anymore," "put your pant leg down to match the other one," "you look like a child," "*grow up!*"

There was a reason the kids loved him, it was because he was mentally their age. He was like that older friend with a driver's license that could take you places and buy you beer. I felt like I had another child that was never going to grow up, rather than a husband. It eventually began causing arguments.

He also had issues with my children. Not in front of them, but he would say mean things that annoyed me and some really hateful things that pissed me off. I was fiercely protective of my children and did not take kindly to someone saying bad things about them. The worst part was knowing the shitty things he said about them, then he'd turn around and act like their best friend to their face.

He thought it was funny to deliberately ignore me and my *"constructive criticism."* I guess I would have to. Personally, I do not like being told what to do as it's a trigger for me that reminds me to be the obedient abused child my mother raised.

He was in and out of jobs and that was a trigger for me, too. He was the polar opposite of my first husband and *nothing* like him, but the not working thing stressed me out. He finally found a job driving a bus and he was good at it. He was a talker and loved people, so it seemed like the perfect fit. He was loving the new job and doing well at it.

Just before our wedding, I had taken a second job delivering papers to pay for the wedding and here I was, seven years later, still doing it. Every day, up at three in the morning to get papers, fold them, and deliver them. He would help on Sundays because Sunday papers were massive. But every other day of the week, it was just me. Joan went with me a few times before she had EJ, but I could not take her after I found out she was pregnant. So, working a second job to make ends meet, plus my regular forty-hours a week job left me feeling resentful. Especially when I would get home from the paper route in time to shower and leave for my real job, only to find him still sleeping soundly in bed.

He had gained a lot of weight over those first few years. I guess I was guilty also as I loved to cook, and he loved to eat but he also loved to eat fast food. When I was at work or a football meeting, he would take my son and his nephew out to eat fast food. He had a "man cave" in the garage where his desk was and one day I needed to find some football paperwork but instead, I found a ton of junk food hidden in his desk and a file cabinet. There was candy, chips, snacks, cupcakes, just a lot of *shit*. I asked him why he was hiding food and he said, "I'm a grown-ass man and I can eat what I want!"

I was pissed at his actions but proud of him for standing up for himself. He did not usually have a voice of his own and was easily manipulated. It used to piss me off that he would do stupid shit just because certain family members did it, like voting. When we first got married, we were discussing the presidential election and he said he was voting for the candidate I was *not* voting for. I asked him why, hoping for but not really expecting a good debate. Tell me what you love about this man's promises and beliefs. But his response was that was who his family was voting for. Wait, what? He asked what I liked about the other guy and I explained my reasons. After a lengthy testimony about the candidate I was voting for, he was like, wow, he is the best candidate. Who knows if he actually voted for my choice over his family's choice, but I wanted him to make *his* own choice, not theirs. I used to say, "Think for yourself." He never could or would do that.

One day, I noticed he had a cough. It was a terrible cough and kept getting worse. So I took him to the ER after I got done with the paper route and he was, in fact, having a heart attack. It was a scary time and I had felt bad for being stern with him about his weight and acting his age. But he was OK and lucky. His cardiologist said he had to drop weight, eat healthy, and exercise. All I could think was, "I told you so," but now was not the time to voice it.

He lost his job driving the bus till he could get cleared by his cardiologist. So here I was being the sole breadwinner, *again*. His job with the bus company was not lost but he could not drive. He had to do bus stop maintenance and cleaning around the shop. Which added up to about four hours a week. He was content; I was not. I was even more agitated after finding more *shit* in his man cave. I was like, "dude, are you kidding me? the doctor said you can't eat this shit." He again said he was a grown-ass man and could eat what he wanted to. I know it was mean and hurtful but I said, "Well, you're gonna be a dead-ass man if you keep eating yourself to death."

I let that settle for a few days and then we discussed it. I said if he wanted to drive again, he had to get healthy. He said he really loved that job. I said, well, it's not enough to support yourself. I would love to have only one job working four hours a week too, but it's not realistic. We are grown adults and have bills to pay; we are not teenagers living with our parents. Everything just kept going downhill from there.

I made a decision to quit the paper route, I was sleeping only four hours a night and killing myself. It was hard to let that money go, but once I quit that job, I realized how much the lack of sleep was affecting me. I did that second job for seven years and I was exhausted. It had been every day, seven days a week, no breaks.

My husband was "looking for work," so he had to use the one vehicle we had during the day. So each and every day, I had to walk to the bus stop to go to work, then ride the bus home and walk back home from the outlets, which were only about a mile but there was a huge hill I had to go over. And I got really resentful every time I would get home after hiking over that hill to find him sitting on the couch, eating fast food, and just playing games in the living room.

Then one day I was fired. *Fired?* I had never been fired in my life. I was very fortunate, though, because I *hated* that job and I got the max on unemployment, which allowed me the opportunity to be picky while looking for my next job. During that glorious time of no work and sleeping in, I was nervous, money was tight and it took everything to cover rent and our phones. There was *nothing* left over. My husband spent his four hours a week paycheck on *shit*, fast food and sugary treats, while I paid the rent and phones and bought healthy food, which was never enough, so I was forced to go to the food bank every Wednesday and wait in a line that would start forming at 3:00 a.m. It was a very embarrassing and humbling experience to stand in a food bank line to get a few bags of free food. But it was necessary to feed my family. It triggered the feelings I had as a child, not getting enough to eat and going to bed hungry. During this awful time, Buster paid the gas, electric, water, and cable bills.

The whole situation *really* annoyed me because my husband told me that his family said that *Buster* was our problem. That he, "my son," was ruining our life and needed to move out and be on his own and see what it was like to pay his own bills. The only response I had for my husband's words were that, "Buster does pay bills and he actually pays more bills than you!" And, "anyone that has shit to say about *my son* because they don't know the facts, can fuck off!" and, "shame on you for allowing someone to say such shitty things about *my son!*"

I was pretty much done at this point. He had said way too many horrible things about my children that I protected them from ever finding out. He was obviously not interested in engaging in our marriage and trying to better himself. It was like having a large child who refused to clean his room. I honestly have to admit that my heart was done long before but I was still trying to make it work. So when he came to me about a week before Christmas and said he had a wonderful idea, I was hesitant when I asked, "what is the idea?" He wanted us to move to Las Vegas. Las Vegas, where his parents lived. His solution was for us to move in with his parents, who hated me.

I said, "Hell, no, I'm not moving to Las Vegas to move in with your parents." He looked wounded and asked, "why not, you don't have a job right now, it's a perfect time to relocate." I said, "No, I'm not moving to Las Vegas. First off, your mom hates me but mostly because my children and grandchildren live here, and there is work here, you just have to find it." He blew up and said that he was going and if I wanted to stay here and support my fucked-up kids who wanted to leech off me for the rest of my life, that it was no longer his problem to deal with. I was shocked and the only word I could muster was, "bye." It was he that wanted us to move in with his parents so he could be rid of my son that was paying all the utilities, yet he felt Buster was leeching off me. Define Irony!

I had scrapped up enough money to buy two Christmas presents, one for EJ and one for Hailey, but that was it. My husband wasn't even sad. I was devastated and felt like a failure. It was the worst Christmas ever, although EJ and Hailey *loved* the Christmas gifts I got for them.

So, two days after Christmas, my husband packed his clothes, his toys, snowboard, RC cars, and video games and he took the one vehicle we owned and off he went to Las Vegas. I had rent due in four days, no car, nothing in savings, no job, and my husband left for Vegas to play, live with mamma, and not worry about bills. All the while talking shit about my son for living with me!

Two days after he left, my phone was turned off. I paid the cell phone bill but they were all in his name. Kinda shitty since I had been dropping off resumes with that phone number on it. Buster's phone was on his plan, too, so Buster went to Verizon and started a new plan for us, never saying a bad word against this man that spoke so poorly of him.

35

Single

Luckily, I got a job pretty quickly and I *loved* my new job. I struggled to get my head back above water. It's very expensive to live on the central coast of California but with my son coming home every payday and handing me his checks, we were able to once again get by. I was so proud that he was so selfless and had no problem giving me his checks. This kid worked so hard for his money and he would come home and give me his signed checks, then ask for twenty dollars of his own money for spending. My guilt was overwhelming, but he wanted to help keep our home. After I started working, he was able to keep his checks and we came up with a good amount for him to pay for "rent," and that was helpful to me to cover rent and bills. He also continued to keep our cell phones on. We were roommates that split the costs. He was definitely not "leeching" off me like my ex-husband claimed. I saved and worked hard and got a new car. My first new car. Life was good.

I was surprised that men were asking me out. I never had self-esteem for as long as I could remember, and thought I was average. My mother had killed any self-confidence and the ability to feel like I was someone with any worth or value. I was not interested in ever having a relationship again. With the exception of my first love, Harold, I obviously had terrible taste in men! My son even told me I was not allowed to choose ever again because my choices sucked! And he was right!

I enjoyed being single, making money, having money in savings, buying my new car, the feeling of freedom, being successful, and not having to deal with a husband who acted twelve years old. I missed my friend but I did not miss being married to him. I had hoped we could stay friends, but he had no interest in that. He was only interested in disparaging my good name by trying to make himself look better. He could not look like the man that left his wife with no job, no car, no phone, and owing rent while he ran off to live with his mamma. I won't even go into the taxes I had to pay off for him because I was married to him.

I never said anything bad about him to anyone, especially to my children, but sadly he did. I still did not tell them the horrible things he said about them and the horrible things he said his family said about them. The saddest part was, it did not have to be that way. We could have stayed friends. Our families could have stayed close but they made it a point to *hate* me because they thought I did him wrong. My children *never* treated his family with hatred and rudeness. I was very proud that I had raised them to be able to consider our blended family members as family, even after a divorce. Harold's family still loved me and *all* my children and we were still *family*. I guess not everyone can be as blessed.

36

Hannah

Buster started dating a girl, Hannah, and I was not sure I liked the idea. I liked it being just him and me. Aside from being messy, he was a great roommate. But Hannah was sweet and won me over. She seemed to really love my son and that made me happy. Every mamma wants the best for her child and hopes and prays for a good spouse who will love him or her. The fact that she was beautiful and creative was just a bonus. Hannah was such a blessing to our family. They fell in love very quickly and before I knew it, she was moving into our house. I enjoyed having her around and we became very close. Hannah had a hard childhood but she managed to escape the chaos of a messed-up family.

She never had her mother around, so she wasn't sure how that type of relationship should be. We talked and talked and enjoyed cooking together and getting to know each other. I loved having her around and felt blessed that she felt comfortable enough with me to start calling me Momma. I gained a beautiful daughter. She was an amazing artist and wonderful cook. I used to love to come home from work and have dinner ready. She and I had a lot in common and we bonded very quickly.

Hannah is beautiful and that alone makes other women feel intimidated. Females can be the worst at passing judgement on other women because of their looks. We, as women, should build each other up, not knock each other down. Hannah was much more confident than I ever was but she wasn't conceited. I think her aunt built her up and, in turn, that gave her the confidence she needed to succeed in life. She was who she was and had no problem calling someone out if they were being a shitty person. She was the most real person I had ever met and I adored her. I think she was just right for my son. She was a strong woman who could help keep him grounded, help him become a better man, husband, and, eventually, father.

THINGS WE SURVIVE

37

Grace, Riley, and Button

We were so blessed the next year with successful pregnancies for all my girls. I felt like God had taken enough of the babies and now it was our turn. My cup runneth over. My girls were all pregnant at the same time. Joan had been trying different things to get pregnant and found out that she had some hormonal issues that made it hard for her to conceive. But there were different things she could try. She was not giving up and she was determined to have another baby. She called me one day and said, "Mom, it worked, I'm pregnant!" I was overjoyed for her. I was overjoyed for me, another grandbaby, more blessings for our family. Now I had to pray for her to carry the baby to term. I did not think she could handle another loss.

Joan had said that she felt like no one even cared that she lost her babies. We were all rallying around

Savannah when Nahla died, but she did not even get a phone call. I told her that no one knew, and we were told after the fact. I said that a miscarriage is painful but different than giving birth to a live baby. I have to *strongly* recommend to *never* say that to a woman who has had a miscarriage. Joan took it all wrong and it upset her.

    She did not talk to me for a while and wouldn't let EJ come visit. It was like someone had ripped my heart out. I loved my grandson with everything in me and it was hard. She also said a few times that she was sick of her family not ever having her back or never supporting her. And that was painful to hear. I have *always* had her back, I have *always* been there for her. When her whole family did not believe her about what Todd did to her, I stood *alone* against them. So we had some history together but I was going to forget all the hurtful shit she did and be as supportive as I could be, because the bottom line was, none of it mattered. She was my daughter and I'd loved her with all of my heart since the day I found out I was pregnant with her. I was always so proud of her strength and courage. It had taken some time and patience to get back to where we were talking freely and I was going to be as supportive of her as she needed me to be.

    The pregnancy went well. Joan seemed really happy and I loved seeing her smiling and happy. She had not had a lot to smile about for a few years. Joan was scared on the day of the scheduled C-section but, like always, the whole family was there to show support and love. Her brother and sister and my dad and me, we may have been overwhelming but we were always overwhelming. Joan gave birth to a beautiful baby girl. We called her Grace and loved everything about her. She was the sweetest little girl and so beautiful. She loved all her cousins and her brother. So the grandbaby count was one boy, four girls, we always count Nahla, too.

Savannah was pregnant with her fourth daughter when Joan had Grace. Riley was a surprise but a blessing, nonetheless. She was a beautiful, quiet little angel. It was a flawless pregnancy and very close after Grace. It was like the opposite of a few years earlier, when the girls lost four babies in two years. Riley had a little spunk and sass and I adored that.

I remember when Buster and Hannah told me they were pregnant. I was thrilled! Hannah cried and Buster looked nervous. I told them what I told the girls, "It's a baby, and a baby is a blessing." It was not my first, it was my *seventh* grandbaby. I had this Nana thing down. I was so blessed to have watched Hannah's pregnant belly grow and even more blessed that I was able to be in the room when my sweet grandbaby number seven arrived. My son delivered my namesake, Juliet June. She was nicknamed Button and it stuck; she was so beautiful and precious.

I remember seeing Buster at fourteen, walking the floor with his nephew EJ at two in the morning so his sister could sleep. I was thinking that someday he was gonna be a good daddy and I was right, my son was an amazing daddy. Button was the youngest of the three we were blessed with in a row. And I remember thinking that these girls were so lucky to be able to grow up together and so close in age.

Joan had been having problems with her husband and she called me the day after Button came home from the hospital. She needed to get out and she needed to get out that day. I've been there; I understood the terror of needing to escape. I knew I had to go and get her and the kids.

I drove the hour drive in about forty minutes. I went to get her to "take her and sweet Grace out shopping." That is what I had to say if asked by her husband. So that went smooth and I felt better when I had her and the baby in the car. What was going on, I asked? "Mom, he's crazy, he shoved EJ so hard he slammed into a door and had bruises." We went directly to the school and took EJ out of school and headed to my house. I was enraged!!!! I had a moment of temporary insanity and actually thought about going back to his house and punching him dead in his face. My heart was breaking for my sweet EJ. How could anyone hurt him? He's the kindest soul and sweetest, most well-behaved child.

Joan told him they were never going back and he seemed relieved but scared. We got to my house and Joan called the police. Now that she was safe in my house with her mom and brother, where she knew that man could not hurt them, she started to cry but her strength came through again and she pulled it together to give the police the full story.

Here we were with my daughter escaping her abuser with her children and we did not have a spare room. But Hannah and Buster agreed that we would do what we had to do to make it work. They had just brought home their newborn and were exhausted but we were *family*.

I remember trying to help Joan get the resources she needed to get back on her feet and be able to support the kids. There were some tensions and understandably so. Joan was traumatized and scared and Hannah was a new mom and had crazy hormones, having just had a baby.

The system is a joke for getting help for abused women. The women's shelter was scarier than what they had escaped from. The Social Services department said there was nothing they could do because she had a place to live, in *my* house. They could not accept that my home was not permanent, EJ and Grace needed bedrooms.

They were sleeping on the couch in the living room with Buster and Hannah's newborn baby up all night. It was not ideal.

We had to work the system, which meant she had to get a hotel room for them so they were considered homeless. And she had to show she had no money in her bank account. Joan was amazing and fought to better her life for her kids. Every day, there was a step forward. She was suffering from PTSD from the abuse she endured in her life and was frustrated with me because she needed something I could not give. I gave her love and support and kept telling her how amazing she was doing, but she needed help with her PTSD.

Even though I had survived abuse all my life, I dealt with it and processed it differently. I survived and felt like *everyone* could do it the way I did, which was to survive, move on, and enjoy the blessings in life. I have learned that *no one* can process abuse the same way. Everyone is unique and everyone has to process abuse his or her own way. Every victim of abuse has different experiences and different situations, so it's impossible for everyone to do it the way I did. I had never talked to a therapist about my abuses and I knew I should probably do so. And, eventually, I did.

Savannah was also going through a divorce and I was so distressed that my poor girls had gone through so much and I just wanted them to be happy. I felt like I had set a bad example in "choosing" a partner. I felt like if I had made better choices, than they would have had a better idea of how to choose a partner in life. I wish I could go back and teach them to choose a man who would make them laugh and cherish them, who would make them their top priority and show them love in everything they do.

I was incredibly proud of Joan. Even though she was struggling and terrified every day, she kept taking the steps she needed to take with me, her private little cheerleader, cheering her on. She got a vehicle, and had to go to classes to get homeless assistance. She was the success story. She got a little house just two blocks from me and that made me and her brother feel better. We could be there faster than 911 if she needed us. She got a job and EJ started in school and we got him registered for baseball, which was so good for him to make friends and have a normal life. EJ and Hailey went to the same school and that was also wonderful for him. Hailey was a social butterfly and knew everyone. Grace was in day care just a few blocks away and I was able to pick her up when Joan could not.

Joan was handling the stress and fear of her ex-husband coming for Grace, which was so intense at times. But then her ex had a seizure and died. When Joan called that evening to tell me, I said, "Joan I don't mean to sound like an insensitive asshole, but problem solved, you're free from that fear forever, you can now move on and have a fresh start."

EJ was active in baseball and football and Joan had her hands full with Grace. Because she did not like crowds, I took EJ to every practice and every game. I certainly did not mind as it was helping Joan out and I wanted to always be there in whatever capacity she needed me. I loved being so involved in my only grandson's life and together we had a lot of fun!

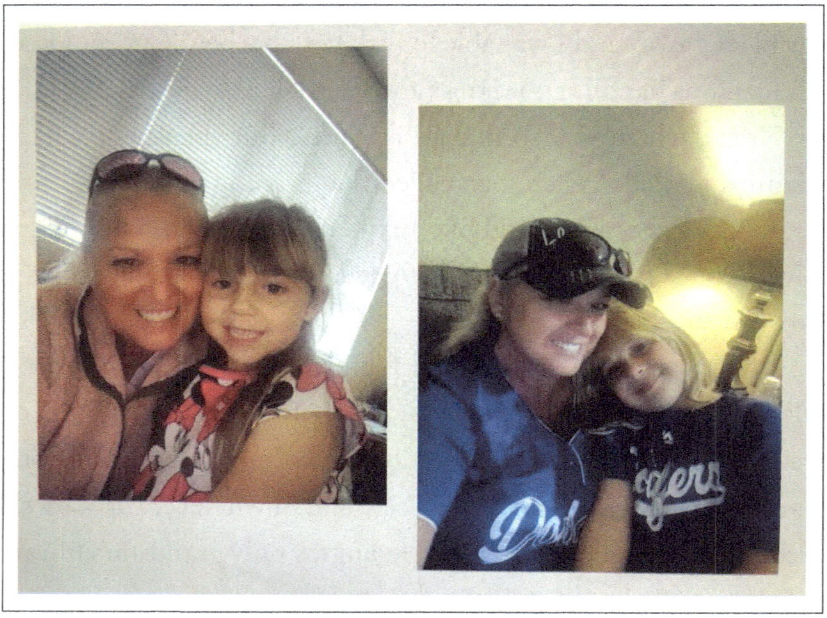

38

When Will I Ever Learn?

What then came as another in a series of poor dating choices, I ended up with another man who was nice, at first, but turned out to be an alcoholic asshole and a bit psychotic! Not sure why I allowed this man into my life, but it was a disaster. He was very controlling and had zero trust in others. I could see the signs, but kept hoping that it would turn around. He then began snooping in my phone, looking for anything that might be evidence of me cheating. Not sure when or why he became so paranoid, but maybe it was a guilty conscience, since he turned out to be married, shocker! another asshole. He would drink and want to fight, he would search through Facebook and ask why men were liking my pictures, my posts, and imply that I was sleeping with them. He actually went back two years on Facebook and asked why a friend had left a certain comment. It became utterly ridiculous and pathetic.

Sadly, I had known hm and his family for fifteen years; he seemed safe. All I can say is, don't think you know people, till you really know people. His sister and her adult children came over for my birthday and then Easter. His nephew and Joan seemed to hit it off. They had known each other since he was eight and played football with Buster. I did not like the idea. I knew things about him, but I could not dissuade Joan or talk bad about him. She was smitten, and I was trying to be supportive.

Things with my boyfriend kept going in circles, as they do with any alcoholic. One night, he got drunk and was acting like he was losing his mind. I was already in bed, asleep, and woke up to him yelling. He had a drill and he kept squeezing the trigger to wake me up. When I awoke and looked at him, he said he was leaving and taking the bed, so I might want to move. I just laid my head back down. The bed was mine and way too difficult to take apart and I knew he was an idiot. He needed to sleep it off.

I finally got up and went to the bathroom. He was yelling and screaming that I needed to make him a priority and clear out the house so his kids could move in. Wait, are *you* not the one who is married? Who has their priorities twisted here? Why would I have my own son, who pays half the bills, move out so your kids could move in?

My son was always good about knocking before entering a room, but he walked in and said, "Mom? You OK? " I told him I was and that I was sorry for the noise and he could go back to bed. But he could not, the asshole had also awoken Hannah and Button. Buster, not convinced that I was OK, left, and the drunk asshole in front of me started back in. He got right up in my face and was screaming. He had backed me up to the bed and I was leaning back as far as I could. My son opened the door with his cell phone in hand and said, "sorry, Mom, but this is *not* happening." He had already dialed 911 and was telling them that there was a drunk asshole threatening his mom and he needed to be removed.

The asshole backed down and went downstairs as the police arrived. I was still in my bed when a police officer came into my room and asked what happened. I told the officer that he was drunk and being stupid. They asked if he had hit me and I told them no. They asked if he had weapons and I said there was a handgun in his nightstand, so the officer took it. I said it was probably best for him to spend the night elsewhere and the officer said that his family was outside with him and they were taking him with them. Thank God, but, wait, his family is here? How embarrassing.

It was then about 1:00 a.m. and I had work the next day, but the house was still clearing out. Once the asshole and his family departed, the police assured me that he wouldn't return and then they left, too. My son and Hannah were now in my room sitting on my bed and we were talking. They were worried and wanted to make sure that I was OK. They had heard him talking shit about me to his kids in the backyard and Buster said, "Mom, any man that will say the shit he said about you and laugh about it with his children, is a sick individual and doesn't deserve you."

He was right, but it was late and I was tired. We all went to bed about 3:00 a.m., but I did not sleep well. I kept having dreams that the asshole came back over to shoot me. I figured he would come home the next day and apologize. But I knew he needed to stay gone. This was a toxic relationship and I did not need another one of those. After getting some sleep, I'd have to figure it out. I went to work the next day, exhausted. I had only had a couple of hours of broken sleep. While I was at work, my daughter Joan called. She was dating my crazy's nephew, so she knew about the night before. I told her I was fine and she told me everything the family was saying about me. *Lovely*!! Again, another man who did not take responsibility for his actions, his behavior, his alcoholism. Maybe that is why he's the way he is because they all enable him.

After I hung up with Joan, my daughter in-law called and said, "momma, he's here!" I asked, if he was sober. I knew Buster was off and home with her and the baby, so they were safe, but I felt bad that they had to deal with the asshole after the night before. Hannah said, "well, he seems to be sober, but he's here with a moving truck and his whole family, and his mom is filming it all with a video camera." Apparently, when Hannah looked confused about the video camera, she was told by the asshole's mom that it was so "we couldn't lie to the police *again*." Wait, when did we lie to the police?

I told Hannah not to worry and not to engage in the insanity. Let him take whatever he was there to take and stay out of the way. So she and Buster stayed out of the way and called me when they were done and gone. All I could think was that I knew I had to get him out of my life but that seemed too easy, and I was grateful! That night, I returned home to find that Buster and Hannah found a couch for the living room and on my nightstand was a beautiful vase filled with sunflowers. I was still unsure why he thought his leaving was going to devastate me; instead, I was filled with relief. It was a peaceful night there alone with no drinking, no yelling, no fighting, and no chaos. Buster, Hannah, Button and I *loved* the calm.

The peace was short-lived, however, as the torture and stalking started shortly after. He claimed we did not break up, he just moved out. Well, in my opinion, when you get escorted out by the police and show up the next day with your whole family, a moving truck, and a video camera for evidence, that is breaking up. If you did not want to break up, you come back the next day with an apology. His leaving was the better option, in my book. He was an alcoholic, married, and insane. I was so much better off!

Once the insanity began, it was long and exhausting. Approximately one month after he left, I woke to find him standing over my bed with a gun. I thought I was gonna die. But instead, he laid down on my bed, put an arm around me, and passed out. Every time I tried to move, he would wake up enough to pull me back to him. I needed to call the police, I needed to get that gun away from him. I was terrified.

After several hours of that terror, he woke up. I asked him to leave before Buster got up and a fight started. He looked confused and left. I watched from my bedroom balcony as he went out to his truck, which was parked crooked in the driveway with the driver-side door wide open. I just prayed it would start and not have a dead battery. He was so drunk, it was a miracle he had not crashed on his way over. It looked like a drunk asshole parked it there. . . I guess one did. How the hell did this man get into my house? This man brought a gun into my home! This man could have killed me and my family, I was beside myself!

I was in such a state of fear, I told the kids that I thought I should move out to protect them. It was over a year of torture. When I was out, he would show up in the same place. He'd send me a picture of the house I was at and ask who lived there and why was I there. I traded in my cars so he did not know what I was driving, only to find out he'd put a tracker on my car. He broke into my house on Thanksgiving and accidentally left his hat on my bed.

He actually called my daughter Joan and asked her if she would go get it before I got home. He told her some bullshit story about going there to shoot himself so I would know how much he loved me. Twisted shit! He was a narcissist; he never would have shot himself. He would tell people we were still together. I even met an incredibly handsome man that he found out about and called him and told him that we were working things out!" That killed any chance with Mr. handsome.

Luckily, my friend and brother by choice, Juan, set Mr. Crazy and his family straight. Juan defines *friendship*. They say a friend is not a friend unless he or she defends you in your absence to others and he did! He has always had my back and I have never doubted it. All the years knowing each other and coaching together, we became close and he is forever my Big Brother. Eventually, Mr. Crazy found someone else to torture and I felt so sorry for her. From that point on, I planned to stay single. After all, how the hell would I explain all the shit from my past to any man that might be interested.

I guess If I could go back and offer my younger self some advice about men, it would be that *you* are enough, you don't need a man to complete yourself. A lot of men are after one thing only and when they get it, they are gone. Don't ever settle for less than wonderful. *Always* trust your gut.

39

Mark

I ran across a friend that I had known for ten years. His name was Mark. I guess he was more of an acquaintance. His son had played youth football and his daughter had cheered, so we knew each other. When we knew each other back then, we were both married. But now we were both single. He was brave and asked me out. I was skeptical. My kids were *not* happy about my decision to go out on a date. But it was lunch, so it felt safe. The day of our first date, I was looking forward to lunch when he sent me a text asking if we were still on. I immediately thought maybe Mr. Crazy had already found out about it somehow and Mark was cancelling. I sarcastically responded, "why are you cancelling?" He said, "no, I actually wanted to see if you wanted to go to the melodrama tonight with me. But you can totally wait till after lunch to decide." I thought that was funny and charming. I said I would roll the dice and say yes before lunch.

So we went on our first and second date the same day. The second date was a bit intense, as it was not just us, it was us and twenty-five of his friends! I felt like it was a screening process. Kinda like what my kids wanted to do to him. His friends were very sweet and we all had a blast.

My children were totally against it. They even requested that I not have their children, my grandchildren, around him. Their reasoning being that they did not want their kids to be a part of another psycho's life. I totally understood and could not fault them for their feelings. My terrible choices in men had affected them. So we never did do anything with my kids, until they were convinced that he was not a psycho. I remember asking Joan, "so am I not allowed to *ever* date again?" She said, "well, maybe after a year and I know he's not a nut job." All I could think was, look who's talking about bad taste in men, but I bit my tongue. Buster was just not even ready to discuss it. Savannah was chill and always wanted me to be happy, so she was willing to meet Mark.

I was in constant fear then that the previous psychotic asshole would somehow ruin it. I talked to my dad about Mark and told him that I did not want Mark to think that I was a crazy woman with my crazy past. Dad sounded kinda hesitant, like my kids did, and said, "baby, *if* this guy is a good guy, then you'd better be open, *full disclosure*; he has to know everything. If Mr. Crazy ever reappears and blows things up, then he will be gone, even if he is the greatest man in the world. That's a lot to ask a man to get over."

So I told Mark *everything*. Surprisingly, he was very understanding and did not run off. We kept going out and doing fun things and became best friends. He was incredibly supportive and understanding. Buster even came around and told me, "OK, Mom, you can date Mark!" Which I found hilarious. Mark taught me that not all men are assholes.

THINGS WE SURVIVE

40

Crushing Revelations

My first husband's mother was diagnosed with lung cancer and, of course, the kids were distraught. She fought it for a while, but it finally became terminal. She and I had just gotten over the past by doing the family's favorite thing, ignoring it. I had harbored anger over her support of her perverted grandson and her saying that I should get over the little spat with Kenny and get back together for the kids' sake. I still participated in family events for the kids till we were informed that, for the gift exchange for the big family's Christmas gathering, that Joan had Todd's *wife* as her person to get a gift for. What? he was out? He was invited and *he was married?* WTF? Has anyone told his *wife* that he is a pedophile? Turns out she had daughters from a previous marriage. Good God, this family was sick and letting this happen *again*. We withdrew and said we would no longer be participating in the Christmas gatherings if a convicted sexual predator was attending. They had to pick *him* or *us* and they chose *him*.

I felt bad that she was sick, but I was not going over there. I did not want to run into the pedophile and "accidentally" shoot him in his balls and go to jail. This is on my list of things I need to repent for. I will *never* be able to forgive him for what he did to my daughter. So, instead, I refrained from going over. I knew Joan wanted to go, so I asked Savannah to go so she could be her sister's guardian. They went to see her and say their goodbyes.

Having not attended the event, I have to report the following exactly how I heard it. My girls were with their grandma, who said to Savannah, "Your dad (Kenny, not Harold) had lots of regrets about what he did." Savannah did not respond and Joan was confused. It did not sit right with her and on their way home, Joan asked Savannah what grandma meant and Savannah dropped the bombshell. My evil, horrible first husband Kenny (Joan's father) had been sexually abusing my oldest daughter Savannah before I kicked him out.

Joan was crushed. Her dad, who was really never there for her and who she grieved for and put on a pedestal when he died, had raped her sister. They talked about it on the drive home and decided to tell me. When they got back, Joan could not bring herself to hear any more, but Savannah told Buster and Hannah and they asked for a family meeting.

I thought, "who's pregnant? I hope it's a boy." We all met at our house and were all sitting in a circle when Savannah, my beautiful baby girl told me what Kenny, that asshole had done to her. I could not process what I was hearing. How, when, oh God, why? I went to the bathroom and puked and passed out. The room was spinning. How could I not have seen this? How could I have let this happen? I wanted to die, (although he was already dead) I wanted to kill him, I hated him. I had once felt bad that he died such a painful death with his liver failure but suddenly it felt like it wasn't painful enough. I wanted to die because my heart hurt so bad. I felt like a complete failure as a mother. If he hadn't already been dead, I felt completely capable of murdering him. I had so much hate and disgust in me, I did not know how to process it. I did not think my heart would ever stop hurting. So much ran through my head, the recollection of times when Savannah just seemed off and I cried for months. His *not* aggressively pursuing the charges against Todd suddenly made sense. He could not go after a sick freak for molesting his daughter when he was guilty of molesting mine.

My former mother-in-law died shortly after this revelation and I was not sure I could go to the funeral. I was sure Todd would be there, and I was not sure I could see him without going off on him. Buster made the decision to not attend his grandmother's funeral. He was certain that if he saw Todd, he would kill him for what he did to his sister. Buster and Joan may fight a lot, but Buster has a strong sense of family loyalty and he loves his sisters. When Todd molested Joan, Buster was just in the first grade and too little to know or understand what Todd had done for many years, but he was an adult now and, the father of a daughter. He wanted to kill Todd, just like I did. Buster chose to not attend the funeral out of respect for his grandfather. He knew he would beat that disgusting pedophile to death if he showed his face and Buster did not want to do that in front of his grieving grandfather.

We discussed this at length and I felt bad for my son. He was robbed of the freedom to attend his grandmother's funeral because a pedophile was going to be welcomed there. We discussed that he would be able to grieve the loss of her in his own way with his loving wife. I told him he did not have to be there for her to know he loved her, she knew that always.

So this meant that I had to attend. I *had* to be there to protect my daughter from that disgusting pedophile. I had to not act on my desires to murder this pig. I had to go, support my daughter, and get the hell out of there! 1 had no clue how hard it would be. I was processing my own pain over what my ex-husband had done to my daughter, trying to understand the pain my other daughter was going through after realizing her father was a pedophile. She must have felt so betrayed by him. He was everything she hated about her abuser.

So here we were at the funeral. We were early and I could tell Joan was nervous. I kept telling her we would pay our respects, hug her grandpa, and leave. She was so brave, like she always was. We walked up and were the first ones there. In front of me was the headstone of my ex-husband who repeatedly raped my daughter. The hatred and anger was overwhelming. I spit on his grave and told him I hoped he was in hell. Not my finest moment, but justified, I think.

As the family started showing up, I was wondering if any of these people knew what sick shit this family hid. This kind woman that they were all here to mourn protected a son who had raped his stepdaughter and beat his wife and she protected her grandson, who was a repeat pedophile. *Why?* I did not understand how any woman could do that.

It was painful to be there and painful to watch Joan, my daughter be in pain when Todd, the disgusting pedophile showed up with his wife and stepchildren. She almost broke down. She wanted to go tell that woman that her husband was a pig. She wanted to shout to everyone there but she did not, for her grandfather's sake. I was proud of her strength. I was always proud of her bravery.

The first couple of weeks after finding out what my ex had done, I puked every day and could not sleep. I just kept thinking about what my baby girl endured. How could this happen in my house and I not know? The only thought that gave me comfort was thinking that the bastard had to be in hell. It was the worst and darkest time in my life, up till then. Even writing about it now is beyond my comprehension.

I felt like a complete failure as a mother. I know now that I wasn't. I know now that I was manipulated by an evil pedophile. He excelled at manipulation and he manipulated Savannah into silence so *no one* knew what he was doing. I had to keep telling myself that. It did not help; the guilt consumed me for a long time. I cried and beat myself up daily. I still have nightmares and I still have days that the tears can't be stopped. The guilt will haunt my head and heart till my last breath.

He got off easy. H was never punished for what he did, he was never exposed for the evil baby rapist he was. He died and escaped any punishment. He died a painful death but not painful enough, in my opinion. This is something I will never be able to forgive.

Joan was withdrawing from the family and I wasn't sure what it was about. I thought maybe she was struggling with what her dad had done. Could it be embarrassment from putting him up on this pedestal after he died, like he was some wonderful father? I also worried that maybe it was her boyfriend trying to distance her from the family. One of the things an abuser will do first is to put a wedge between the victim and his or her family.

His family hates my family! Me, obviously, because of the breakup with his psychotic uncle. And they hated Hannah. I'm not sure why, because Hannah never had any kind of relationship with any of them. She tried to be kind when they were all over at *her* home, but they treated her like she was an unwanted guest rather than my daughter in-law who lived there and who I loved.

They had all been over one day for a barbecue. Button had been sick with an ear infection. Everyone was being extremely loud and Hannah had come downstairs and asked if we could all keep it down a bit, she had just put Button to sleep. For some reason, that pissed them off. They all said she was rude, but she wasn't, she was exhausted. Joan's boyfriend's sister even said out loud to where I heard her, "Someone's bitch is showing." I looked directly at her and said, "No. . . someone's sick baby is asleep!" She hated me after that, too, but I did not care. Talk about a bitch and rude as hell. His sister *hated* Hannah. I'm not sure why, other than that she was jealous. Hannah was beautiful, happily married, and confident. His sister was *not*. She was not beautiful and was extremely overweight, and had no self-esteem. She was one of those hateful, nasty, bitchy girls I spoke of earlier.

I'm pretty sure this negative talk about Hannah was said in front of Joan, and she started repeating it as well. It was frustrating to me because I knew Hannah well and I understood her and loved her. I knew she was a wonderful person and, if given the chance, most people would love her. Could she be bitchy? Absolutely, but who isn't a bitch from time to time? I know I can be a bigger bitch than Hannah.

Things between my kids were getting really bad. As a mom, it's really hard to watch your children fight, especially over ridiculous shit. They all needed to get back to what was important, *family*. There were outside influences from outside sources that did *not* have the family's best interests at heart. It's like watching a scary movie and you see the killer hiding in the closet and you want to scream, "He's in the closet," but you can't, it won't do any good. If

I defended one of my kids because I *knew* for a fact that what he or she had "heard" was bullshit, then that child would get mad at me and claim I was picking sides. I wasn't. They were all wrong. They all had hurt feelings over stupid shit said in anger or sarcasm, and stupid shit that *other* people were saying. The hardest part was listening. If one was talking about the other, they all forgot that that is still my child you're talking about. What you're saying is hurting my heart. I want to be supportive but you're breaking my heart. And everyone was doing it.

    I get it, it's hard when your siblings say something hurtful but I just wanted my children to take a step back and see all the chess pieces on the board and get back to loving and supporting each other. When they were little, I could send them to their rooms or make them apologize or make them hug till they laughed. But when they are adult children, all the childhood rules no longer apply, damn it. Too bad we can't have them listen to their mamma *forever*.

41

Birdie Belle

During this hard time in our lives, with all my kids fighting, we did have the blessing of another grandbaby. My son, Buster and Hannah, my daughter-in-law welcomed grandbaby number eight, Birdie Belle, and she was just as precious as her big sister, Button. So, the count was now one boy, seven girls, and one happy Nana.

My son had two baby girls and he was killing it! He was a great girl dad. His little Button was so much like him, stubborn and smart. She had her daddy wrapped around her little finger. He adored Button and I knew he would do the same with baby Bird.

Birdie was a beautiful addition to my little tribe of blessings. I was very upset that Joan was not speaking to Hannah and Buster at this time and missing out on her niece. Button called Joan her *ammie*, because she could not say *auntie*, and was missing her, Grace, and EJ. Grace and Button called each other "best friend." They truly loved each other, and I know some of their happiest times were when they were together.

I was sad that Grace was missing out on her little cousin. Grace had the sweetest heart and *loved* babies. Her day care provider sent a picture of her one day that was the most precious example of Grace's kind heart. The day care provider had gotten a four-foot statue of a ninja turtle and Grace was trying to hand it a toy she wanted to share with it. She thought it was another child. It melted my heart. That is my Grace's heart.

I was enjoying the new baby and watching Button be an amazing big sister. Birdie was such a sweet baby and so full of smiles and love. Buster and Hannah were amazing parents and adjusting to life with two little ones. Buster was a very hands on dad, the minute he would get home, he would jump in and help Hannah. Some days, they would build blanket forts and spend the day on the floor with the girls. I was impressed that these two had turned out to be so good at parenting. Hannah did not have stable parents growing up and her mom had disappeared. Buster's dad was, well, horrible and abusive. So the fact that they were so good at the parenting thing made me proud.

I remember Buster coming to me and asking me, "momma, how did you do this alone? It takes me and Hannah both to handle these kids. I could not imagine doing it alone!" I was so pleased that my son was *not* like his father. I was *really* grateful that he had not grown up to be abusive. That had been a fear since he was little. He had his dad's blood and resembled him, but he was all me. Thank God.

THINGS WE SURVIVE

42

Brain Surgery

Savannah had been dating a real jerk. I could see the abusive personality and I could see him causing her to distance herself from her family. He was putting ideas in her head about her family members. I could tell it was just a matter of time till that man hit my daughter. I hated him and it was killing me to bite my tongue. She was convinced he was wonderful and that was one battle that could never be won.

One day, she called and sounded weird, like she was not making sense. She said she had been to the hospital the night before because she thought she had a seizure, but they were taking too long so the loser boyfriend took her home. They were out of town and decided to drive home. She called to tell me that she was home but something did not sound right in her speech. So I went over there to check on her. Something was wrong! I told her I wanted to take her back to the hospital here and I told the loser that she needed to see a doctor and I was taking her to the hospital. He was annoyed and said that the doctor saw her last night and she was fine, but I was taking her whether he liked it or not.

I took her to the local hospital that I knew was best for brain issues. After her evaluation and gathering reports from the previous hospital, they came in to tell us she had had a brain aneurysm and they were transferring her by ambulance to Cottage Hospital in Santa Barbara for emergency brain surgery. I called the asshole and he said, "she's fine, huh, just like I told you." I said, "no, she's not fine. She's had a brain aneurysm and they are transferring her to cottage hospital for emergency brain surgery." Then I added, "she never should have left the hospital last night and she could have died!" He did not care; he just did not want to be out of town in a hospital with my daughter.

They prepped her for the transfer and I made a couple of calls. I called my kids to let them know. Even though they were all fighting, I knew they would want to know because, bottom line, they do love each other. I called my best friend, Peggy. Having been through something similar when her daughter Kallie was twelve, I needed a reassuring voice to tell me it was going to be OK. Instead, she said, "swing by here before you leave; I have something for you to take." I felt bad, it was late and I really just wanted to get to the hospital.

The ambulance got there and loaded her in and off they went. I drove like a scared mom over to Peggy's and she hopped in my car, apparently, she was going with me. I felt bad, I did not know how long I would be there. I figured Peggy could always take my car home and I could get her to come back or call a family member to come get me. Either way, there was no telling her no, thank God, because I was terrified.

We made the hour-long drive to Santa Barbara. She was very comforting and a wealth of knowledge. She had been in this situation before with Kallie. The hospital had Savannah stabilized for the night and were planning the surgery for the next morning. They were doing all her prep while we waited for the morning to come. It felt like the longest night ever. Peggy and I talked and laughed, I don't think I could have endured that alone. She was my rock. They told us what they were going to do, which was to go in through her femoral artery and up to her brain to place a coil and a stent. I was exhausted and trying to wrap my head around the information. How are they going to operate on her brain through her leg? Modern technology is amazing.

They ended up having a lot of other surgeries to do and she kept getting bumped, so when they finally took her in for surgery, it had been thirty-six hours. I was exhausted, but it was finally time. Peggy and I went to eat. I did not want to leave the waiting room, but Peggy insisted that we eat. She said we weren't going to miss anything and she was right, I felt better after we ate.

Savannah's surgery went well. She was in recovery and I felt relieved. After she was in her room and stable, Peggy and I started making plans. Savannah was going to be there a few days, so I was going to take Peggy home and check in with work and *sleep*. We had been awake for fifty-six hours.

I can't say enough about Peggy and what her being there for me during that time meant. She is the most selfless person I have ever known. She would do anything for anyone without hesitation and the world is a better place because she is in it. I am so fortunate that she is my best friend.

I wasn't surprised that her asshole boyfriend never came to see Savannah and thought that I would have a heart-to-heart talk with her after she recovered from her surgery.

I was pleased that Buster and Hannah had been concerned about Savannah and were going to extend the olive branch and try to reconnect. Hannah was going to bring her dinner. This was a glimmer of hope for my momma heart and it was a start that my kids were going to mend the broken fences that were kicked down by outsiders. Now, if we could get Savannah to see that her boyfriend was an idiot, then we could all try to get Joan to see the same about *her* loser boyfriend.

Two weeks after Savannah's brain surgery, I got a weird text from her. The text simply read, "Help 911 come now!" I had literally just gotten home after having dinner with Mark and had changed into my pajamas. I tried to call her as I was getting redressed. No answer, so I tried to call her oldest daughter, Hailey, and again, no answer. I was still trying to reach one of them as I grabbed my shoes and headed down the stairs. I got to the living room and must have looked distraught. Buster looked at me and said, "what's wrong, Momma?" I told him about Savannah's text and that I could not get in touch with her or Hailey. Hannah immediately said, "go with her, Buster." I was so relieved that my son was going with me. We both continued calling her and Hailey, with no luck. Her house was just over a mile away, but it felt like it took forever to get there. We got to the intersection just before her house; the light was red and we saw flashing lights around the corner. My heart sank. My phone rang and it was Savannah's best friend, Marissa. She said that she was out in front at Savannah's and the police were trying to get in. She said Hailey had messaged her that the asshole boyfriend was beating her mom up.

My heart stopped. I relayed that info to Buster and he said, "Run this light, Mom." We got to Savannah's and there were several police cars there. They were standing on her porch trying to gain access to the house. Hailey was peeking out her window and asked if she could come out. I told her to stay in there till the police knocked on her door. I asked where her sisters were. She said she had taken them in her room with her and she had her door locked.

I recognized one of the officers as Peggy's son-in-law, Kallie's husband. I yelled out to him, "Matt, she just had brain surgery!" At this point, I did not know if my daughter was dead or alive. It was the scariest moment of my life. It felt like it was taking forever for them to get in there and I had no idea where Savannah was. I could hear the loser arguing with the officers. Matt called down and asked if he had weapons. My heart stopped, oh, my God! Yes! This asshole has guns. If she is not already dead, is he going to kill her? Is he going to harm my granddaughters? Is he going to come out shooting?

All I could do was cry and keep assuring Hailey that it was going to be OK, even though I did not know if it was ever going to be OK again. I was so proud of her. She heard it start to happen and she got her sisters huddled in her room and locked the door. Hailey had gotten a message from her mom's friend, asking if she was OK. Marissa had received a weird text from Savannah like I had and was worried that Savannah was having another brain aneurysm. She kept trying to call her, but Savannah was not responding. So Hailey told her what was going on. Marissa said she was on her way and to call 911. Hailey called 911 and that is why she was not answering.

I later found out that Hailey had been on the phone with 911 and she was clear and calm and so helpful to the police. She was telling the police what she was hearing and she could hear her mom crying and whimpering. At one point, she said she could not hear her mom anymore and thought she was dead. She was keeping her sisters safe and quiet. She was afraid he was going to come in there and hurt them. I can't imagine the fear that she was going through at that point. But she still continued to be strong and brave.

I was out front waiting with my son. Hailey's dad had arrived, along with Marissa and her mom. I could not believe that this was happening. Why had I not said something to Savannah sooner? Would she have even listened to me. I should have tried. I paced and prayed for God to protect the girls and to please keep my daughter alive. It was killing me that they could not get in. What if she was dying while we were all standing around?

A paramedic pulled me aside and asked about Savannah's medical history. I was able to tell him about Savannah's recent brain surgery and her medications. He got the name of her neurosurgeon and called it in to have someone call and have her records sent to the hospital they were going to transport her to. It was the hospital I had taken her to two weeks prior. So I told him that as well. They were all prepared to take care of her if they could just get to her.

There was a commotion at the front door and the officers saw an opportunity to gain entrance. There was yelling and we were reassuring Hailey it was almost over and to be strong. It was like time was in slow motion. It took about twenty minutes till an officer came down, it was Peggy's son-in-law, Matt. He told me that Savannah was alive and that the paramedics were getting her ready for transport. He warned me that she had been beaten very severely and to prepare myself. Just then, they brought the asshole down and I thought Buster would kill him. I wanted to! They put the loser in the back of a police car and Buster told him what a punk he was. He was lucky that the police were there to protect him from Buster.

Then the paramedics brought down my baby girl. She had bandages wrapped around her head; they covered her whole head and one of her eyes. She could not see me but she called out for me,

"Mom." I could hear the fear in her voice, looking for her Momma. I could not help but start sobbing, she was alive! That asshole failed and she was alive! I said, "I'm here baby, it's gonna be OK." They finally let me go to her and I took her hand and cried as quietly as possible.

She was bleeding so bad and it appeared her teeth were broken. She had blood coming out of her mouth and obviously somewhere on her head because it was all bandaged. Her brain surgery had left her unable to see clearly out of her right eye and that was the eye that was not covered. She could not see me but could tell I was crying. She asked, "How bad is it, Mom?" I lied and said, "It's not that bad, baby, you're gonna be fine." She knew I was lying! I do not lie very well and she could always tell if I was not being truthful. She said, "Mom, you're lying!" Then I could not contain the tears; the damn was broken, and I laid my head on my beaten, broken, bleeding, child's leg and she put her hand on my head and said, "Mom, it's OK. . . I'm alive. . . I love you. . . please don't cry."

I was relieved when they told me I could ride to the hospital with her. By the time they had her loaded in the ambulance, the bandages were soaked through with blood. She was on blood thinners from her recent brain surgery, and the asshole who just beat the shit out of her had split her head open and she was bleeding to death. They drove with lights and sirens and it still felt like it was taking too long. I had to ride up front, so I called her sister and told her what had happened. She was obviously upset and worried. I told her I would call and fill her in when I had news. I called Mark and told him where I was and what happened. He was stunned. I had just told him at dinner the overwhelming feeling I had that the asshole was going to eventually hit her. I could not believe this was happening! I thanked God for protecting my precious granddaughters, for protecting my daughter from being killed! I thanked God for giving Hailey the courage and strength to save her mama's life. I wanted to kill the asshole! This is another thing I can't *ever* forgive.

The emergency room was chaotic. There were police and victim witness advocates, doctors, and nurses; it was overwhelming! I kept looking at my daughter and looking at her bruises and gashes. I could tell she put up one hell of a fight and all I could think was *good girl*! *Fight till you can't fight no more!* I was so proud of her strength. An incredible strength she obviously passed on to my granddaughter. They were incredibly brave women and I was proud to call them mine.

I had to listen to her complete statement to the police and it was painful to hear what she endured. He had come home drunk and mad. Mad that her ex had volunteered to bring them a Christmas tree for the girls. Mad for no good reason other than because he liked to be drunk and mad. She said he kept getting up in her face and she *knew* he was about to snap. She sent her friend Marissa a text and me the 911 text. She said he came in and smacked her phone out of her hand and the beating began. She swung and fought and kicked till she could not see. It was apparent by the bruises on her hands and legs and I was convinced she had broken bones, fighting for her life!

She passed out briefly and came to and could not see. Her good eye was swollen shut and her other eye was swollen almost shut but she could not see out of it anyway. The blood was pumping out of her because of the blood thinners she was taking due to her brain surgery. Her head was split open and the bleeding was constant. She said she crawled to the bathtub as he was threatening that if she ever told anyone about this, he would kill her.

She said her hands kept slipping and she was confused as to what she was slipping in. It was her own blood. She kept trying to feel for a towel to wipe it up. She made it to the tub and he turned on the shower and threw a towel at her, telling her to clean herself up. With every word of her statement, I was getting more and more angry! He was psychotic! What a worthless man to beat a woman this bad. Men like that are not *men*, they are disgusting *punks* and deserve the same to be poured out on them.

When she was finally released from the hospital that same night, we went to my house so I could pick up my car and her spare key. Buster and Hannah were asleep, but Savannah went straight up to their room. They both sat up and saw her face and began to cry. She crawled in bed with her baby brother and sister-in-law and they hugged and cried together.

It did my momma heart good. They had been torn apart partly by that asshole and his lies and were not even speaking two weeks prior, yet here they sat, all the anger aside, all the bad things that were said and all the bad melted away and there was nothing but love. The love of family.

THINGS WE SURVIVE

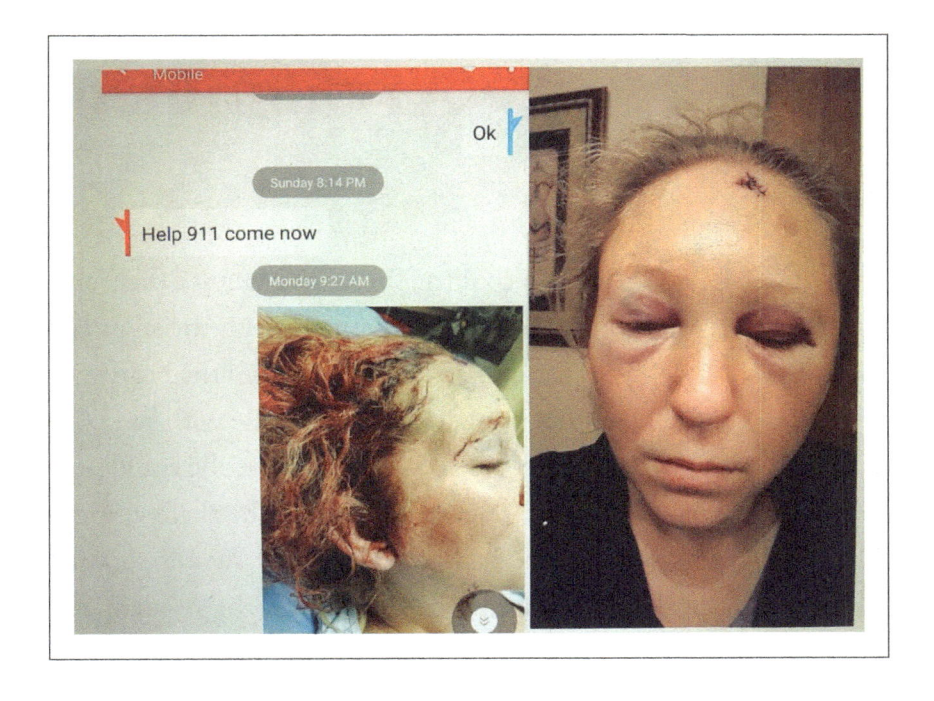

43

Aftermath and Arraignment

Savannah could not be alone when she first came home. Luckily, the surgery with the stent and coil was not compromised from the beating at the hands of that punk, but she had to be with someone at all times. The doctor was worried that she could possibly have another seizure. So I would be there at night after work and she had her family and friends rotating days. People brought food and things she needed. She was very blessed with family and friends.

We had a court date for the losers' arraignment and Savannah looked awful. The blood was all cleaned off but the bad bruising had started. One eye was swollen shut and the other eye was just slightly open but she could not see out of it due to the brain surgery. She had stitches on her forehead and scalp. Her eardrum was ruptured so the beating as a whole, compounded with the brain surgery, left her equilibrium way off. Due to the blood thinners she was on, she was so bruised it actually hurt to look at her.

We got her ready the day of the arraignment and she needed help to walk but she stood tall and walked into that courtroom to face the animal that did this to her. Everyone starred as we walked into the courthouse and courtroom. I was grateful she could not see that far and could not see the look in people's eyes. I got her seated and held her bruised hand as they brought the prisoners in. The corrections officers were *amazing*. They stood in front of her, blocking his view. I didn't want him looking at my daughter. He was asking for bail and stood there and told the judge that he was *not* a violent man and he was a disabled veteran and yadda yadda, lie, lie, lie. It was making me want to puke. The DA replied saying that the defendant's victim was in the courtroom and as he said that, the officers parted so the judge could take a look at my baby. The DA said, "you can see how violent this man is, your honor, by looking at his victim's face. He's a threat and needs to be remanded." I thank God the judge agreed. The look on the judge's face when he saw my baby told me he was a dad and probably had a daughter.

The loser was staring at Savannah and it pissed me off. I felt like a mama bear wanting to protect my cub and reach out and pummel this asshole who tried to kill my child. He had the nerve to mouth, "I'm sorry." I could not contain myself"; I said, "No, you're *not*! You're a punk!" Then the officers closed back in formation in front of my daughter, protecting her from the stares of the punk who tried to murder my child. As we were leaving, I thanked the officers for what appeared to be a few good men wanting to help me protect my baby. We had a lot of appointments with the victim witness department and the DA that day and the days that followed.

The DA met with us one day and told me that they were going to charge him with assault only. I was pissed. The man tried to murder my daughter and you want to charge him with assault? Why not attempted murder? He *knew* she had just had brain surgery just two weeks prior and he made the decision to pummel her brain. She was going to have a long road to recovery in front of her and they wanted to charge him with *assault*? A charge that would carry only a three-year sentence. I asked the DA if this was his child, how he would feel about it? He told me, "Steph, I am a father and I totally understand your frustration, but I can prove the assault all day long, everyone *knows* he's guilty but him. However, attempted murder is harder to prove and if we fail, he walks. If we want him in jail for any amount of time, we have to go with assault." So there it was, three years and he's out in eighteen months. *Disgusting*! Our criminal justice system is so broken in California.

I honestly wanted, plotted, and dreamed of luring him to Savannah's. Then, when he got there, I would shoot him after taking a baseball bat to his head and every limb. I wanted him to suffer like my daughter had. I totally understood temporary insanity because I was insane with anger and that anger took a very long time to get over. I don't dream of murdering him anymore, but I still don't know if I will ever forgive him.

44

Siblings

That first week after Savannah's assault, I was at her house and she and Hailey were asleep on an air mattress in the living room. Her assault took place in her bedroom, so it was hard for her to even go in the room. Plus, the mattress was soaked with her blood. Hannah and Marissa had come over and cleaned up the house and all the blood. Hannah even put a new shower curtain and rugs in the bathroom and threw away the ones that were covered in blood. Savannah's bedroom and bathroom looked like a murder scene from a movie. But Hannah and Marissa managed to get it clean, everything but the mattress.

Savannah, Hailey, and I slept in the living room. It was comforting to see my brave, fearless warriors sleeping peacefully together and safe where I could protect them. About two days after the assault, Savannah and Hailey were snoozing on the air mattress. I was watching a movie and my dad called to check on Savannah. He got the update and I could tell something was up with him. I asked what was going on. He paused and said that his cousin had contacted him and said she found a woman online who was searching for her biological father. Her bio dad had the same name. And she was from the town my dad was from. He recognized her mother's name. I asked him what the woman's name was. As he was telling me this, I searched for her on Facebook and found her immediately. My sister, Piper!!!

I typed out a private message that read, "Hello, my name is Stephanie Carr and my second cousin said she saw online that you were in search of your biological father and my father has the same name. He is from the same town and he said he knew a woman with your mother's name. If you are the one in search of Joseph Carr, I am your sister."

Before I hit *send*, I told Dad that I found her on Facebook and asked if I could send the message. He seemed a bit nervous and said, "what if she doesn't want to hear from me?" I asked why would she be looking for him if she wasn't interested in hearing from him. He agreed and I hit *send*. We were chatting about his memory of this woman he knew after my mother and before he was with my sister Dorothy's mom. About twenty minutes later, I received a reply.

Savannah had heard the entire conversation and was now sitting up, looking curious, when I said, "Dad, I got a reply." He asked, "what did she say?" I read her reply: "Oh, my goodness, I have been looking for him forever, I am so happy to have found you." I was crying, Savannah was crying, and I asked Dad if I could give her his phone number and he said yes. About five minutes later, very stoic, he said, "your sister Piper is calling me." I said, "Oh, my God, go talk to her and call me back." What a blessing it was at such a dark time in our life. Over the next few weeks, we all got to know each other through Facebook and phone calls. Piper lives in New York and came out shortly after to meet her new family.

It was an awesome visit and we clicked like we had been raised together. I thought Piper looked like me and it was kinda weird how similar our separate lives had been. We all got together, all of Dad's girls, me, Piper, Dorothy, and Lindsey. And I am so pleased we got a picture of Dad with all his girls. As we were all sitting together, Dorothy asked, "OK, Dad, so I'm going to ask the obvious question that we are all thinking, 'Is there anything else we should know about?'" We all laughed and Dad said, "not that I know of!"

On Piper's next visit out to California, she brought her son, Forrest. He and Buster hit it off and have become great friends; I love that they have a bond like they were always raised together.

I feel so blessed with all of my sisters. Dorothy and I started off as best friends, then found out we were sisters. We have always had that bestie bond and can talk about anything. We have the bond of loving our baby brother, Joseph. Losing Joseph was devastating for us. I always wanted to be smart and beautiful like Dorothy and I'm blessed that she is not only my sister, but still my dear friend.

Jeffi is not one of Dad's daughters, but he loves her like she is and she loves him, too. Jen and I went through some dark days together and so many blessed days as well. She just happened to be there with me when Buster was born. We have a very close bond that I am sure is from being raised in the same household and enduring similar experiences. We survived together.

Piper and I, although we just met, have this connection and are so similar. I think it might be that I was the first one to reach out to her. Or maybe just that we do have the same blood. It took us more than fifty years to find each other, but here we were, blending our families.

Lindsey is the youngest; I was fourteen when she was born. And even though there is a huge age difference, we are close. She used to come over to the beach to hang out for vacations and holidays. She and Savannah were only two years apart, so they sometimes seem more like sisters, but I love their friendship.

I have had moments of pause where I wonder, with all that support, why I never shared with them that I was being abused by my first husband. I guess I was embarrassed and ashamed. Looking back, I have so much regret that I did not lean more on my sisters. I know that reading this will be the first time they hear about what I survived. Jeffi and my baby brother, Jason, knew about the abuse from my mom, and Jeffi knew of the abuse from our grandfather, as she was his victim as well. But none of my other siblings knew.

I have such a weird family dynamic that most people would have a hard time keeping up with. My dad and mother were never married to each other but were both married a few times, so I have brothers and sisters who are not related to each other. Which brings to mind my brothers. I have four *"real"* brothers and a few honorary brothers who have always had my back.

Samuel is the oldest and on Mom's side, the brother who was so mean to me. After I moved away, we did not have a lot of contact, just when we happened to be at one of our families' functions, birthdays, or funerals, but other than that, we did not speak. He was not kind and lied a lot and never missed an opportunity to spread lies about me. I'm certain that was one of his favorite pastimes. Although, since I left my mother's house, it did not elicit the beatings it did when I was there with Mother. But it did not stop him from speaking poorly of me. I found it weird that we had not spoken in more than thirty years, and yet, he still would manage to find shitty things to say. I understand now that he was a miserable person, and that is what miserable people do. That is exactly why I distanced myself from him. He died and it did not affect me in any way. It was like someone had told me a stranger had died.

Joseph is from dad's side. He was my dad's mini-me. He was a handful, but precious! I remember meeting him when Dorothy and I were "best friends." She called him pesky, and he was, aren't all brothers? But when I went to California the first time, he was *my* brother, too. Dorothy shared him and the three of us had the best summer! When I had my babies, he was an *amazing* uncle and he loved my babies. Joseph never liked my first husband, Kenny. He used to say, "There is something off about him, sis!" At first, I just thought he was talking shit, like dad. But I later realized that Joseph had a sixth sense about his sisters, like dad did.

When I first got back to California right after Kenny had exited our lives, Joseph called. He wanted to come back to California. Thank God was all I could think. He and Dorothy had always been so close and she had been talking to him about returning. She setup a bedroom for him at her house in Walnut Creek and got him a train ticket. While we were talking about him coming back, he said he wanted to come see us when he got settled and maybe even move to Pismo eventually, and I was excited. The day he was supposed to leave to come out here, Dad called and told me, "We lost Joe." I immediately thought that maybe he ended up in Alaska or something weird. I asked Dad, "Where did he end up?" Dad said, "Steph, he died last night!" I have no words to explain the pain and sadness of losing my brother. That was such a sad time for us all. I miss him every day and cherish the thoughts I have of him in heaven with my grandbabies and Harold.

Jason is on Mother's side. He is the brother I am closest to. He was in the back seat when my mother dropped me off at dad's, naked. He is a gift from God to me. He has always been there and even though he lives in Wyoming, he loves to surprise me by showing up for a week-long visit, and I *love it!* Jason loves all my sisters, even the ones he is not technically related to. He has a kind heart and a forgiving soul and is a blessing to our family. My children and grandchildren adore Uncle Jay.

Justin is my brother through Sharon. She had him when she and dad met, but he is my brother. He and I were always close and I adored him. He was a good kid and grew up to be a good man and a good father. We are not in constant contact anymore as we are both busy with our own lives, but he is always my Baby Brother.

THINGS WE SURVIVE

45

Losing Joan

Since Savannah's assault, I sensed Joan growing further and further away. She *hated* her brother Buster and Hannah and seemed to hate me, too. It was heartbreaking for me. I was constantly being yelled at by her. She would send mean, hateful texts that were short and expressed her anger with me.

One day, I was shopping in Walmart when I got a call from the mother of one of EJ's best friends. She was in town for the weekend and had a hotel room at the beach and invited EJ to come spend the weekend with them. She asked if I could take him over there and I said, "Sure, have you cleared this with his mom?" She said yes and I said OK, that I was shopping and running errands but as soon as I was done, I would go get him and drop him off. She told me what hotel they were staying at and we hung up.

Within five minutes, I received a text from EJ, asking if I could give him a ride over there. I told him I could as soon as I was done with my errands. About five minutes after that, I got a message from Joan asking why I thought I was EJ's mother. Confused, I asked her what she was talking about. She asked why I was using EJ's friend's mom to manipulate time with him. I said I wasn't, and was really confused. She asked how long we had been planning this. I told her I had no clue that they were in town and I wasn't planning anything. I was annoyed and tossed my phone in my purse, checked out, and got in my car. I looked at my phone and there were more texts from Joan saying to just be honest and tell her what I had planned, then one saying "*hello?*," and a third saying, "Don't try to come up with a fucking bullshit story, that is why you aren't responding. I'm not a fucking idiot, Mom."

I was in shock. What the hell is happening and why is she so angry with me? I responded that I was not ignoring her, I was at the checkout in Walmart and I wasn't making up any story. I did not know EJ's friends were in town. I already had plans for the weekend and I was not even going down to where they were. Then I asked if she still wanted me to take EJ down there. She said, "No, and as a matter of fact, you can come pick up his phone. I am getting him one on my plan and you won't ever have his new number." My only thought was, WHAT THE F***!!!!!! I was heartbroken and confused. What the hell happened? Why am I the asshole in her eyes? I have been nothing but loving and supportive to her and her kids since birth. I wasn't sure what to do. She wasn't really speaking to anyone at this point but me. My fear was that her loser boyfriend and his family had finally turned my daughter against me.

I did not really know what to do, so I laid low for a while. I knew that she had Grace's dance recital coming up and I figured we could chat after. About a week later, I got a call from EJ's friend's mom, who asked if I was coming up for EJ's birthday party. I had no idea that they were having a birthday party for EJ. Rather than tell her about what had happened with Joan, I apologized and said I had no idea about EJ's party, but that I already had plans and I told them to have a blast. I was heartbroken, I was going to miss my first grandbaby's birthday, the first one ever missed by me.

Since they returned to the Five Cities area, I was EJ's ride everywhere. Joan, at first, was scared to leave the house or to leave Grace because she was fearful of her husband trying to kidnap her. I *get that* and did not mind. I love my grandson with every ounce of me, like I do her and all my other kids and grandkids. I would do anything for them and her. I took him to every baseball practice, every baseball game, every football practice, every football game. I would pick Grace up from daycare on Fridays and anytime Joan needed me to. I was very involved with her family. So to go from every day to *nothing* was a shock and heartbreaking.

The day of Grace's dance recital finally arrived, and I went. It was good to see my grandson out front and I hugged him. I told him I was sorry for missing his birthday party. I asked him what he wanted for his birthday gift and he said a baseball bat. I sat with my former sister-in-law, Jackie, and my stepdaughter, Krystal. We all laughed and talked and took pictures. After the recital, we went out to see Joan and Grace. As Joan was walking up to us, I put my arms out to hug her and she purposely dodged my hug and walked past as she said something to Jackie. Krystal noticed and said, "awkward," as I was standing there with my arms out to hug my daughter and apologize for whatever I did to piss her off. I felt like I'd been punished enough for whatever I had done. My heart was broken. I gave Grace the flowers I had brought for her, hugged her, and went home and cried.

I called my dad and talked to him. I was crushed and missing my daughter and EJ and Grace. What the hell does she think I did? Whatever I did wasn't bad enough to be extracted from her life *forever*. I never could have done anything bad enough to lose them.

Joan's grandmother had called her a liar and said that her abuser, Todd, was "just curious," and she still loved her and allowed her in her life. Todd's mom had threatened both of us and she was still a part of Joan's life. Her father had abandoned her but she forgave him without an apology and deeply mourned him upon his death. Her stepfather had called her a lying slut who stole painkillers and he was allowed to be in her life. Whatever she thought I had done, I would apologize for and move on, even if it wasn't true.

Grace's birthday celebration was a couple of weeks later, and I went. I *know* Joan did not want me there, but I was with my dad and I knew she wouldn't uninvite him. It was awkward and uncomfortable but I was able to hug and kiss my grandbabies and give Grace her gift.

I sent the kids cards for Halloween but they were returned in the mail. My heart was crushed worse than it had ever been. I did not sleep. I would wake up feeling like I was suffocating. I spent more than six months not sleeping more than a couple of hours without waking up gasping for air, dreaming of my daughter, EJ and Grace, dreaming of being together with them, dreaming of taking them away, dreaming of what I could have possibly done to deserve this pain.

It did not make any sense to me, no matter how many times I went over it in my head. Nothing I'd said or done could justify her wanting me out of her life forever. I cried a lot and I would pray every day for God to soften Joan's heart and make things right. I would look for the kids every time I was out in public, praying I would see them and get the opportunity to hug them. Then that thought would make me cry again. Without physically stopping, my heart hurt more than anything I can express. It was a suffocating, horrible pain and the *worst pain ever*!

I knew I had to talk to someone, so I did. It did not help but it did make me realize that I wasn't crazy, even though I felt like it. I was prepared to reach out and planned how to go about it for months. The only thing I could think of was that Joan's loser boyfriend had told her something terrible. I prayed every day for God to open a door for me. I went through every emotion during this time. During my "angry" phase, I changed my password to "ILoveJellyBean#1," just to remind myself every day that I did love my daughter but was hurt by her actions.

I had got them all Christmas gifts, so on Christmas day, I reached out and sent her a text that I loved her and missed her and the kids and that I hoped they'd all have a wonderful Christmas. *Big mistake*! She spent the next two hours texting what a horrible mother I was. She said I was disgusting, and that, basically, I was calling EJ a liar and that I was calling her loser boyfriend a liar, too. The horrible things she called me crushed me and left me feeling broken. I felt like asking her if her intent was to hurt me, and if so, then she had succeeded. I finally had to set my phone down. The only other times in my life that I'd been spoken to so hatefully were by my mother, by both my husbands, and by Todd and LeeAnn's mom. You would think I would be used to it by now but coming from my own daughter was crushing!

It was the worst Christmas I'd ever had. When my other kids, who loved me, came over, I was trying to hold it together. I was cooking and sobbing. Buster wanted to see the texts, but I wouldn't let him. The things she had said were so mean and so hateful and included him, Savannah, Hannah, and baby Birdie. I decided to never let anyone read what she wrote. I'm her mom and I can forgive her anything because of that. There is nothing more powerful than a mother's love and the ability to forgive is unmatched, except for God's love and His ability to forgive. I saved her texts just in case I needed to show her or prove she actually said the disgusting shit she said to me on Christmas, but through therapy, I am almost ready to delete them. Almost.

That Christmas was rough and losing Joan, EJ, and Grace was the hardest thing I have ever gone through, and I've been through some hard shit. But because of my family and my other children and sweet grandbabies, I survived it.

My sweet Savannah told me months later that Joan had said she was mad at me because I was "talking shit about her with Buster and Hannah in front of EJ." I was confused. I don't remember sitting in a room with them and verbally bashing her, especially in front of EJ. Have I talked about her or listened to them vent about her? Yes, absolutely, but I've usually been the one defending *her*. But I have also sat in a room *with her*, talking shit about each one of them, Buster, Hannah, Savannah, and her ex-stepfather. She is the *worst* at talking shit, but guess what? That is what family does. They get mad at each other and talk shit and get it out and move past it. They *forgive* and grow from it. It's usually a good time to find out who's lying, because it's usually the outsiders. So if you ask, "Hey, asshole, did you say yadda yadda," and they say, "Ummm, no, who told you that?" You quickly uncover the lying shit stirrer.

Savannah also told me that Joan blames me for what Kenny did to Savannah, she feels like I should have known. If she only knew that I blame myself, too. I have spent years regretting not leaving him when they were little. I have spent more hours hating myself for that than she ever could.

I've recently learned that Joan's loser boyfriend has been revealed to be the asshole I said he was, *shocker*! I would hope that whatever he said about me to her would now be rethought. I remember her texting me that fateful Christmas, asking if I was calling him a liar. Well, yes, he was and I wanted to ask her, when have I ever had a conversation with him? And why would I tell him something so bad to warrant getting written out of your life *forever*?

I know there will be a time when I see my EJ and Grace again. My dad has always said that kids are smart and they know the difference between bullshit and whipped cream. They will one day *know* that I love them, no matter what they have been told. They are gonna know that I have missed them so much that I thought my heart would stop, and some days wished it would. They are gonna know that no matter what, their Nana loved and missed not only them but their mom, because family is the most important thing next to love.

My prayer is to one day have my daughter back in my life.

46

Family First

After many months of healing, Savannah was getting better and stronger and I was happy that she was so strong and brave; I was honestly in awe of her. How did I raise such an amazing woman and, in turn, how did she raise such a brave, fearless warrior like Hailey? I had always felt weak and fearful, but somehow I raised this incredibly strong woman. Savannah and I have always been close. I was blessed with the gift of this beautiful soul and I have known she was a blessing since I was given her on Christmas Day all those years ago. She blessed me with four more blessings through her girls. I love and cherish the times we get together. It's chaos when we are all together, but I feel nothing but blessed.

I love our deep conversations and friendship. It wasn't always as effortless as it is these days. I know any woman with a teenage daughter can understand this. I loved the phone call from Savannah that started with, "Mom, I'm so sorry for every mean word I ever spoke about you and to you and I thank God you did not kill me when I was a teenager...not sure how you did not, but thank you!" We laughed and I reminded her that she had two more coming up who would be teenagers at the same time. She sarcastically thanked me for the reminder of that hell to come.

She has helped me so much through the heartbreak of losing Joan, EJ, and Grace and has kept in touch with her sister and keeps telling me to never give up on her and I won't. But I am so thankful for her unconditional love and support through the whole thing and, really, all her life. Savannah is the kindest, loving, most understanding person I know. She is not judgmental or spiteful and I know her dad would be so incredibly proud of her strength and her kind heart. She reminds me a lot of Harold.

Buster is another one of the greatest blessings I have. He is the most faithful, protective, and loving son a mother could ever ask for. I have no doubt in my heart or mind that he would protect me to his death if he had to. He would have been a dream son for any man and I was sad that he *never* had a father to see all his accomplishments. I was just happy that I was always there for him. I got to see every touchdown and amazing tackle or fumble recovery, every celebration with football teammates. Also, every game-winning shot in basketball and every incredible sneaky turnover. He was such an awesome athlete and I felt blessed to have witnessed it all.

His sense of humor and witty personality is so much fun to be around. If more men were like my son, the world would be a much better place. It's hard to raise a good man, but I think I nailed it! He proves that every day in the kindness he shows others and in the father he has become. He makes me proud daily!

He brought an amazing blessing to the family with the choice of his wife, Hannah. She is an awesome daughter and mother to my sweet Button and Birdie. Hannah defines *family first* and has always had Buster's back and mine, as well, and that is a quality I adore and appreciate. She also loves her nieces and nephews with her whole heart and without hesitation would do anything for all of our family. I could not love her more if she were my own flesh and blood,

My sisters are incredible; during the Covid pandemic, we all banded together. Dorothy started a Facebook page for us sisters to keep each other up to date and help support each other. My sister Jeffi was feeling alone and sad and I asked Dorothy if we could add her to our page and she said, "Of course!" She also added one of our sister Piper's sisters. Even though we are not all related to one another, it's our "Sister Tribe" and such a supportive blessing for us all. We may not all share the same blood with each person, but we are *family*.

It brings to mind something my parents said: "The more people that love your children, the better off your children will be." That works for our crazy family. Most importantly, the more people that love you, the better off you will be. And one thing our family has been blessed with is love.

47

Lessons Learned

How do I summarize fifty-two years of life lessons in just over fifty-seven thousand words? I guess I will talk about the lessons; I've learned so many of them. There have been some dark days in my life, but I'm not unique. I have known a lot of people with similar tragic stories. I have known some people with worse tragedies in their life. But for me, I had to focus on the beauty in my life, my children, my grandchildren, my dad and mom, my sisters and brothers, and my true friends and loved ones. There is so much beauty in my life.

No matter what awful things life throws at you, you can either choose to let that ugliness define you and drag you down and make you miserable all the time, or move past it and *live*. Live a better life than what you survived. Don't take the ugliness with you. Always believe in *love* and *family*, that alone can get you through any dark evil thing that this world may throw at you. And yes, there is still a great deal I must forgive, that I must move past, but, I no longer carry these things with me day-to-day.

Although many of the lessons come from the painful times I've overcome, I choose to focus on the blessings in my life. Through those lessons, in the blessings and because of my faith in Christ, *I have survived!*

Philippians 4:13 - *I can do all things through Christ who gives me strength.*

Cherish everyday like it's your last
Forgive, even if it's not deserved
Love your people with all your heart
Cherish the love you receive
Be brave
Be strong
Know that you can't fix anyone
Don't beat yourself up for what other people do to you
Be true to *you* and thank God every
day for your blessings

Stephanie Carr

Have you ever wanted to write a book, share a story, or reflect on the journey lived? My sister has done just that, she has found a way to shine a light into the dark corners of her life and share with the world her story of trauma, abuse, and betrayals. Her prayer is to encourage others to step forth out of the darkness they are currently facing and to step into the warmth of being a survivor; creating a new joyous life filled with love, a beautiful family, and blessed friendships—a life of abundance.

Stephanie has built that life for herself and is now sharing her journey with the world. My prayer is that this story finds its way into the darkness of those lives now struggling with their own hidden horrors, to that heart that has no escape from the unspeakable abuse, to the person that believes they are confined to their current situation. To find that person or child that pre-Covid had the escape of school or work but now find themselves trapped in a "cage called home."

Please visit the author's website at www.stephaniecarrauthor.com, go to our Contact Us page, and share how this book has touched your life. All submissions will be considered for our *Abuse to Abundance Anthology*—publication date to be announced.

— Dorothy M. Carr, Founder
Ocean's Edge Press

Looking for Immediate Support:

Here are some national resources—their services can provide local contacts.

Rape, Abuse & Incest National Network Sexual Assault Hotline

1.800.656.4673 | www.rainn.org

National Child Abuse Hotline

1.800.422.4453 | www.childhelp.org

National Domestic Violence Hotline

1.800.799.7233 | www.ndvh.org

National Teen Dating Abuse Helpline

1.866.331.9474 | www.loveisrespect.org

References:

1. Bipolar Disorder - Wikipedia as of 11/19/2020

Made in the USA
Coppell, TX
31 March 2025